手绘名物系列
Hand-Drawn Classic Travel Landmarks

中国古镇

Ancient Chinese Towns

刘颖 文
Written by Liu Ying

潘英赵 译
Translated by Pan Yingzhao

赵楠 黄泽鑫 绘
Illustrated by Zhao Nan and Huang Zexin

中国画报出版社·北京
China Pictorial Press · Beijing

图书在版编目（CIP）数据

中国古镇：汉英对照 / 刘颖文；赵楠, 黄泽鑫绘；
潘英赵译. -- 北京：中国画报出版社, 2023.4
（手绘名物系列）
ISBN 978-7-5146-2069-6

Ⅰ. ①中… Ⅱ. ①刘… ②赵… ③黄… ④潘… Ⅲ.
①乡镇—介绍—中国—汉、英 Ⅳ. ①K928.5

中国版本图书馆CIP数据核字(2022)第042807号

中国古镇（汉英对照）

刘颖 文
赵楠 黄泽鑫 绘

出 版 人：方允仲
项目主持：方允仲　齐丽华
责任编辑：齐丽华　李聚慧
英文翻译：潘英赵
英文编辑：陈星宇
责任印制：焦　洋

出版发行：中国画报出版社
地　　址：中国北京市海淀区车公庄西路33号　邮编：100048
发 行 部：010-88417360　010-68414683（传真）
总编室兼传真：010-88417359　版权部：010-88417359

开　　本：16开（787mm×1092mm）
印　　张：14.75
字　　数：150千字
版　　次：2023年4月第1版　2023年4月第1次印刷
印　　刷：北京汇瑞嘉合文化发展有限公司
书　　号：ISBN 978-7-5146-2069-6
定　　价：128.00元

前言

本书是"大美中国"书系中的一本。顾名思义,所谓"大美",无外乎自然界和人类社会中,具有高度审美价值的客体、对象。它们可以是自然界中的山川河流,可以是花鸟虫鱼,也可能是风雨雷电、莺歌燕舞,更有可能是通过色彩、线条、声音、文字等人文艺术表现出来的各种艺术形式,如音乐、舞蹈、建筑、书法、绘画、雕塑、戏剧、电影等。而这些,都来源于东方古老的文明大国——中国。

浑浊而奔腾不息的黄河孕育了古老的华夏文明。中国人的先祖从母亲河走来,由部落壮大成为部落国家,从王国跨越到帝国,经历了漫长的封建时代。最终,在近代的数次实践之后,中国走上了社会主义新中国的道路——在这漫长的历史中,有统一,也有分裂;有强盛,也有衰败。部落演进为国家的历史,中国经历了一千多年,封土建国的周朝,前后存在了八百多年,之后漫长的封建时期,历时两千余年才告结束——可中国的历史,却又不止于长:不仅长,还富于变化。中国五千多年的文明和国家史,从来不是一成不变的:在四千余年的建国史中,中国经历了约十五个朝代,六七十个政权交替更迭,更见证了不计其数的大小战争——战争和政权更替固然给人民带来了深重的灾难,却又在客观上催动着社会生活方方面面的变化,为中国展开了一幅波澜壮阔的历史图卷;从天文、历算到农耕器具的进步,从造纸、印刷到选官制度的变化、商业的繁荣,中华民族就这样一步步走来,走到今天。

Foreword

This book is part of the "Beautiful China" book series. As its name implies, the book series focuses on depicting objects of high aesthetical value in nature and human society. They include not only creatures such as birds, beasts, insects and fish but also natural phenomena such as wind, rain, thunder and lightning. They may also be various forms of art composed with colors, lines, sound and texts, such as music, dance, architecture, calligraphy, painting, sculpture, drama, and movie. Regardless of their form, all of them derive from China, an ancient civilization in the East.

The muddy, ceaseless flow of the Yellow River fostered the ancient Chinese civilization. Nourished by the "mother river", Chinese ancestors gradually developed their tribes into tribal nations, then kingdoms and empires across the feudal era. Eventually, after several attempts of practical exploration in modern times, China embarked on a path of socialism with Chinese characteristics. Throughout its long history, China experienced unifications and separations as well as ups and downs. The history of tribal nations in China lasted for more than 1,000 years, followed by the Zhou dynasty (1046-256 BC) that spanned about 800 years. Then, China entered the feudal period as long as more than 2,000 years. However, the course of China's history is more than just long; it is also full of changes. Across its history of more than 5,000 years, the Chinese civilization has never stopped the pace of evolution. Throughout its history of more than 4,000 years as a nation state, China fostered 15 dynasties and some 70 regimes, and underwent numerous wars. Of course, wars and regime shifts might bring grave disasters to the people, but at the same time they accelerated changes in all aspects of society and composed the eventful picture of Chinese history. From progress in astronomy, calendrical science and farming tools, and improvements in printing and papermaking techniques

习近平主席曾多次指出,"当今世界正经历百年未有之大变局";正是在这样的时代机遇和文化背景下,中国外文局责成中国画报出版社推出了"大美中国"这个书系。本书系既是对中国自然、风物、人文的总结,也是为了向全世界关心中国、热爱中国、崇敬中国的人讲好中国故事。

但凡讲故事,必要有一个主题,有一个入口;我们选择向世界展现中国之美,这并非任意为之。人们总是喜欢美好的东西,这非但是中国人民的追求,也是全世界各国人民、各个民族的追求——不同文化对美的定义或许不同,可这追求却是一致的,而且古来有之。

中国之美既有历史的深邃厚重,又有地域的辽远广阔。大到富丽繁华的都市,小到鲜有问津的村镇,历史总会在这里那里,留下星星点点的痕迹。地域的辽阔又为中国之美赋予了不同的风格。我们既有高山大川,又有小桥流水;既有高屋广厦,又有陋室闲庭;既有"长河落日圆"的雄壮,又有"清泉石上流"的清丽……疆土有多少寸,美就有多少种,简直是说也说不尽的。以自然地理和城镇乡村为依托,我们更想展现一种人文的厚度,南北东西、平原山地、沿海内陆……不同地方的人,

and official selection systems to prosperity of commerce, the Chinese nation have constantly moved forward step by step to the present day.

Chinese President Xi Jinping said on many occasions that the world is undergoing "profound changes unseen in a century." Facing such historic opportunities and cultural context, under the instruction of China International Communications Group, China Pictorial Press presented the "Beautiful China" book series, which not only reviews the natural and cultural sights of China but also tells China's stories to global readers who care, love and admire China.

A story needs a theme or a topic. We do not casually choose "Beautiful China" as the theme of the stories we try to tell. All people love beautiful things. In fact, the pursuit of beauty represents the common aspiration of not only the Chinese people but also people from other parts of the world. The definition of beauty may differ for different cultures, but people around the world have had a shared aspiration for beauty since ancient times.

The beauty of China stems from its profound history and vast territory. Whether in spectacular, prosperous metropolises or in nondescript small towns, we can always find clues left by history. The diverse cultures scattered around the country's vast territory bestow on China different types of beauty. There are high mountains and big rivers as well as exquisite bridges and murmuring streams; there are skyscraping buildings as well as simple dwellings; there are magnificent views of torrential rivers in the setting sun as well as elegant sights of clear streams flowing through rocks… The beauty of China is just as boundless as its territory. With this book, we would like to show readers the natural geography and cultural profundity of various cities, towns and villages across China, from plains to mountains and from coastal areas to inland areas, as well as how people in different regions live in

他们都在以什么样的方式生活着,他们的生活有何不同,而这种种生活又如何共同构成了中国的文化和民生的一部分。一言以蔽之,我们想要传达的,不是某种抽象的概念,不是简单的意象或标准化的符号,而是由真实、具体的细节所构成的鲜活的生活与生命。

本书系通过文图作品讲述中国故事,以画面语言为主,辅以文字的叙述、解释和说明,向读者传递更完善的印象和更系统的知识。

除了摄影作品,我们还将绘画艺术融入到书系当中。例如"手绘名物系列",我们选择了通过水彩画的方式去讲述城市及其民俗的故事,这不仅构成了对城市的刻画,同时也是一次上好的艺术和美学教育。选择水彩画这一既为亚洲也为欧美所熟悉的艺术表现形式,去讲述城市这一最为大多数人所熟悉的生活空间,这是由于我们想以此作为出发点,把中国故事讲好,走近听众,把故事讲得生动真实、可闻可感。

沿着这样的轨迹,我们希望把中国最美的一面展示给世界,也想把中国的故事讲给全世界每一个喜欢她的人听。

different ways and how their lives together compose the country's diverse cultures and lifestyles. In one word, we intend to reveal the vigor of life through true and specific details, rather than an abstract concept, a simple imagery or a standardized symbol.

This book series tells stories about China through vivid pictures and language. Therefore, it prioritizes images, supplemented with textural narrations, explanations and remarks, so as to enable readers to obtain deeper impressions and systematic knowledge.

In addition to photographic works, we also incorporate painting into the book series. For example, the "Hand-Drawn Classic Travel Landmarks" sub-series feature hand-drawn watercolor illustrations depicting cities and their folk customs. This is not only an ideal way to portray cities, but also provides a chance for art and aesthetic education. Watercolor is a form of art familiar to readers around the world. We chose this form of art to portray cities, a kind of living spaces familiar to most people, in an effort to tell China's stories in a vivid, perceptible way and make them closer to readers.

By doing so, we hope to show the most beautiful side of China to the world and tell China's stories to every reader who is interested in the country and its culture.

目录 Contents

前言 Foreword

第一章 Chapter 1
江南水乡
Waterside Towns in the South of the Yangtze River

浙江
Zhejiang

01 乌镇：枕河而居，先锋江南
　　Wuzhen Town: Living by the River and a Pioneer in the South of the Yangtze River....002

02 西塘：烟雨长廊，梦里西塘
　　Xitang: Dreamlike Xitang with Promenades Shrouded in the Misty Rain 004

03 南浔：中西合璧，园林宅第
　　Nanxun: Garden-Like Mansions where the East Meets the West 006

04 石浦：山城渔港，海钓天堂
　　Shipu: Fishing Port and Marine Angling Paradise..................008

05 前童：清溪绕舍，诗礼儒乡
　　Qiantong: Clear Streams Around Houses in a Culturally Prosperous Town..................010

06 廿八都：百姓古寨，文化飞地
　　Nianbadu: Ancient Fortress and Cultural Enclave 012

07 俞源：太极星象，文运昌盛
　　Yuyuan: Astrology of the Supreme Ultimate Indicates Cultural Prosperity 014

08 郭洞：风水福地，长寿之乡
　　Guodong: Land of Fengshui Geomantic Omen and Longevity 016

江苏
Jiangsu

09 周庄：方圆双桥，水乡之最
　　Zhouzhuang: Waterside Town with Twin Bridges and Enchantiing Scenery 018

10 同里：繁华富土，醇正水乡
　　Tongli: Prosperous and Intoxicatingly Pure Waterside Town 020

11 甪直：五湖六泽，三步两桥
　　Luzhi: Five Lakes, Six Marshes, and Two Bridges within Three Steps..................022

12 木渎：园林古镇，秀冠江南
　　Mudu: Ancient Town of Gardens, Being the Best of the South of the Yangtze River ...024

13 锦溪：碧荷长堤，莲池古桥
　　Jinxi: Long Embankments Lined by Green Lotus Leaves; Ancient Bridges amid Lotus Ponds...................................026

14 千灯：炎武故里，昆腔绕梁
　　Qiandeng: Hometown of Yanwu and the Land with Reverberating Music of Kun Opera..................028

15 惠山：二泉映月，泥人纳福

　　Huishan: Spring Reflecting the Moon and Clay Figurines Bringing Fortune 030

16 洞庭东山：碧螺春醉，洞庭橘红

　　Dongting Dongshan: Intoxicating Biluochun Green Tea and Red Tangerines of

　　Dongting 032

17 震泽：吴头越尾，蚕丝之乡

　　Zhenze: Hometown of Silkworms at the Junction of the Wu and Yue States 034

18 盛泽：丝绸之都，衣被天下

　　Shengze: Silk Capital Benefiting the World 036

19 溱潼：水乡明珠，青砖绝响

　　Qintong: Pearl among Waterside Towns with Exceptional Brickwork 038

20 朱家角：沪上名镇，船拳之乡

　　Zhujiajiao: Famous Town in Shanghai and Hometown for Boat Boxing 040

第二章 Chapter 2

徽派民居
Huizhou-Style Residential Buildings

安徽
Anhui

01 宏村：浓淡相宜，画里乡村

　　Hongcun Village: Picturesque Village Appealing with Either Light or Heavy Make-up......044

02 西递：诗礼桃源，民居典范

　　Xidi: Poetic and Ritualistic Land of Peace and Happiness and Model of Folk Residential

　　Buildings 046

03 卢村：木雕楼群，徽派精华

　　Lucun Village: Buildings with Wooden Carvings, Reflecting the Essence of the Huizhou

　　Style 048

04 南屏：巍巍祠堂，幽幽曲巷

　　Nanping: Lofty Ancestral Halls and Tranquil Winding Lanes 050

05 屏山：青山画屏，古桥落虹

　　Pingshan: Green Hills Looking Like Painted Screens and Ancient Bridges Resembling

　　Fallen Rainbows. 052

06 关麓：亦儒亦商，翰墨书香

　　Guanlu: Land of Scholars and Merchants amid Cultural Fragrance 054

07 呈坎：负阴抱阳，国宝之乡

　　Chengkan: Home of National Treasures amid Well-Balanced Yin and Yang 056

08 唐模：水口园林，风姿天然

　　Tangmo: Estuary-side Garden with Natural Graceful Bearing 058

09 棠樾：慈孝无双，牌坊之乡

　　Tangyue: The Hometown of Memorial Arches with Unparalleled Love and Filial Piety 060

10 查济：桃花流水，别有天地
　　Zhaji: A Different Land with Peach Blossoms and Flowing Water..................062

11 三河：江淮水乡，土菜飘香
　　Sanhe: Waterside Town with the Fragrance of Local Cuisines in the Yangtze-Huaihe River Valley 064

江西
Jiangxi

12 瑶里：瓷源茶乡，林海雪瀑
　　Yaoli: Cradle of Porcelain and a Hometown of Tea amid Forest Seas and Snow Waterfalls 066

13 富田：碧血丹心，红星闪耀
　　Futian: Patriotic Heart like a Shining Red Star 068

14 流坑：科甲联芳，千古一村
　　Liukeng: Famous Village for All Eternity with Multiple Successful Candidates of the Imperial Civil Examinations at the Highest Level..................070

15 理坑：山中邹鲁，理学渊源
　　Likeng: Mountainous Land like 'the Hometowns of Confucius and Mencius' and the Place of Origin for Neo-Confucianism 072

16 上清：道教福地，南国仙都
　　Shangqing: Blessed Land of Taoism and Fairy Capital of the South 074

第三章 Chapter 3

彩云之南
Yunnan — South of the Colorful Clouds

01 大理：苍洱毓秀，风花雪月
　　Dali: Well-Endowed Cang'er amid Romantic Themes..................078

02 双廊：南诏风情，水天一色
　　Shuanglang: Nanzhao's Local Conditions and Customs amid Natural Sceneries Featuring the Sky and Water Merging into One Color 080

03 沙溪：茶马古道，千年集市
　　Shaxi: Ancient Tea-Horse Road and Millennium-old Market 082

04 凤羽：百鸟朝凤，文武有道
　　Fengyu: All birds Paying Homage to the Phoenix and a Land with Well-Balanced Cultural and Martial Achievements 084

05 大研：丽江王城，古乐悠长
　　Dayan: The Royal City of Dali with Lingering Ancient Music..................086

06 束河：清泉之乡，雪山倒映
　　Shuhe: A Hometown of Clear Springs with Reflections of Snow-capped Mountains...088

07 鲁史：茶叶之乡，马蹄铿锵
　　Lushi: A Hometown of Tea Leaves amid Clanging Hoofbeats..................090

08 建水：滇南邹鲁，文献名邦

Jianshui: A Southern Yunnan Land like the Hometowns of Confucius and Mencius and a Famous Land of Literature 092

09 和顺：滇南侨乡，绝胜苏杭

Heshun: An Overseas Chinese Hometown in Southern Yunnan, with Its Landscape Better than those in Suzhou and Hangzhou 094

10 黑井：千年盐都，灵源普泽

Heijing: A Millennium-old Salt Capital with a Spiritual Source and Widespread Benefits..096

第四章 Chapter 4

巴山蜀水
Mountains and Rivers in Sichuan

四川
Sichuan

01 阆中：阆苑仙境，巴蜀要冲

Langzhong: Fairyland Dwelled by Immortals and Strategic Location of Sichuan 100

02 丹巴藏寨：千碉之国，美人如玉

Danba Tibetan Villages: Land of Thousands of Watchtowers and Jade-Like Beauties 102

03 李庄：长江重镇，人文荟萃

Lizhuang: Strategic Town Along the Yangtze River with Rich Cultural Heritage 104

04 尧坝：川黔走廊，伞韵涵芳

Yaoba: Sichuan-Guizhou Corridor, with Its Umbrellas Revealing Appeal and Fragrance ...106

05 福宝：青山福地，天人合一

Fubao: Blessed Land amid Green Hills Featuring the Unity of Heaven and Humanity 108

06 洛带：客家名镇，会馆之乡

Luodai: Famous Hakka Town and Hometown of Guilds 110

07 罗泉：千年龙镇，保路救国

Luoquan: Millennium-old Dragon Town, Protecting the Roads and Saving the Country ...112

08 仙市：盐道明珠，天上街市

Xianshi: Pearl on the Salt road and Market in Heaven......................................114

09 黄龙溪：天府仙境，火龙灯舞

Huanglongxi: Heavenly Fairy Land with Fire Dragons and Lantern Dances 116

10 龙华：八仙立佛，凉桥卧波

Longhua: Standing Buddha Statues on the Eight Immortals Mountain and Cool Bridge Lying above the Waves 118

重庆
Chongqing

11 龚滩：乌江画廊，绝壁古镇
   Gongtan: Gallery-like Land along the Wujiang River, with Exceptional Walls of an Ancient Town...120

12 龙潭：民族风情，人杰地灵
   Longtan: Ethnic Conditions and Customs on Remarkable Land with Outstanding People......122

13 中山：山居菁华，桫椤王国
   Zhongshan: Essence of Living in a Mountain and Kingdom of Cyathea........................124

14 涞滩：蜀中二佛，瓮城巍峨
   Laitan: Second Buddha in Sichuan with Towering 'Urn City' 126

15 万灵：巴渝古寨，移民水乡
   Wanling: Ancient Village in Sichuan and Waterside Town of Migrants.........................128

16 西沱：千里盐道，云梯登天
   Xituo: Thousand-Mile Salt Road with Scaling Ladder Reaching Heaven.......................130

17 双江：双溪绕城，忠烈遗风
   Shuangjiang: Twin Streams Around the City with Legacy of Loyalty and Martyrdom 132

第五章 Chapter 5

湘黔胜景
Wonderful Scenery of Hunan and Guizhou

湖南
Hunan

01 凤凰古城：田园牧歌，最美小城
   Fenghuang Ancient Town: Most Beautiful Town with Pastoral Scenes.........................136

02 芙蓉镇：王者之地，银河落天
   Furong Town: Land of Kings with Waterfalls Like the Milky Way Falling from Heaven......138

03 德夯苗寨：苗疆明珠，飞瀑流纱
   Dehang Miao Village: Pearl in the Miao Ethnic Group's Territory with Cascading Waterfalls like Flowing Silk Yarn..140

04 里耶：秦简故里，湘西名镇
   Liye: Hometown of the Bamboo Slips Used in the Qin Dynasty and a Famous Town in Western Hunan 142

05 张谷英村：民间故宫，耕读继世
   Zhangguying Village: Forbidden City in the Folk Passed on Generations by Farming and Reading...144

贵州
Guizhou

06 镇远：山雄水美，龙舞端阳
   Zhenyuan: Majestic Mountains and Beautiful Rivers with Dragon Dances on the Dragon Boat Festival 146

07 肇兴侗寨：鼓楼之乡，侗歌飞扬
   Zhaoxing Dong Village: Hometown of Drum Towers with Reverberating Songs of the Dong Ethnic Group 148

08 青岩：山地兵城，状元故里
   Qingyan: Military Town in the Mountainous Areas and Hometown of Successful Candidates of the Imperial Civil Examinations at the highest level 150

09 岜沙：远古遗风，枪手部落
   Basha: Customs Handed Down from the Remote Antiquity in a Tribe of Firearm Holders 152

10 郎德上寨：英雄故里，苗歌嘹亮
   Langdeshang Village: Hometown of Heroes with Resonant Songs of the Miao Ethnic Group 154

11 西江：千户苗寨，芦笙之乡
   Xijiang: Miao Village with Over 1,000 Households and Hometown of the Reed-pipe Wind Instrument 156

12 旧州：且兰古都，长征足迹
   Jiuzhou: Ancient Capital of Qielan State, with Footprints of the Long March 158

第六章 Chapter 6

北方古韵
Antique Appeal of Northern China

山西
Shanxi

01 平遥古城：华夏文明，晋商遗韵
   Pingyao Ancient City: Land of Chinese Civilization with the Lasting Appeal of the Shanxi Merchants 162

02 碛口：黄河古渡，龙吟碛口
   Qikou: Ancient Ferry Crossing with Dragons' Chanting 164

03 张壁：明堡暗道，星象奇村
   Zhangbi: Open Castle with Secret Passages and Extraordinary Village Corresponding to Star Signs 166

04 静升：灵石江南，三晋大宅
   Jingsheng: Great Mansions in Lingshi (Comparable to the Areas South of the Yangtze River) of Shanxi 168

陕西
Shaanxi

05 党家村：民居瑰宝，不染纤尘
   Dangjia Village: Treasure of Residential Buildings Without a Speck of Dust 170

06 青木川：山中桃源，乱世传奇
   Qingmuchuan: Mountainous Land of Peace and Prosperity with a Legend During Turbulent Days 172

北京
Beijing

07 爨底下：京西山村，北国幽谷
   Cuandixia: Mountainous Village in the West of Beijing and a Secluded Valley of Northern China 174

河北
Hebei

08 鸡鸣驿：塞北邮驿，古道沧桑
   Jimingyi: Post Station Beyond the Great Wall with Ancient Roads of Vicissitudes 176

09 暖泉镇：古堡金花，逢源暖泉
   Nuanquan Town: Golden Flowers in an Antique Castle with Smoothly Flowing Warm Spring Water 178

河南
Henan

10 朱仙镇：中原名镇，忠义相传
   Zhuxian Town: Famous Town in the Central Plains with the Transmission of Loyalty and Righteousness 180

11 赊店镇：皇城气派，铁旗商魂
   Shedian Town: the Demeanor of an Imperial City and the Merchants' Soul with Iron-Firm Flags 182

山东
Shandong

12 新城镇：半朝王家，四世宫保
   Xincheng Town: Filling Half of the Imperial Court with the Wang Clan Members, with the Fourth-Generation Imperial Protector 184

第七章 Chapter 7

岭南风情
Local Conditions and Customs of the South of the Five Ridges

广西
Gangxi

01 兴坪：奇山秀水，景甲天下
   Xingping: Beautiful Mountains and Rivers amid Its Best Landscape in China 188

02 黄姚：千年诗集，梦境家园
　　Huangyao: A Millennium-Old Poetry Collection amid a Dreamlike Home..................190

03 扬美：左江明珠，融汇南北
　　Yangmei: A Bright Pearl Beside the Zuojiang River, Fusing the South and the North..192

广东
Guangdong

04 赤坎：中西合璧，古埠侨乡
　　Chikan: Ancient Commercial Port and Hometown of Overseas Chinese with an Integration of Chinese and Western Elements 194

05 沙湾：金声玉振，飘色粤韵
　　Shawan: Land of Piaose Art Featuring Guangdong's Appeal and Sounds of Gold and Jade 196

06 大鹏所城：海防要塞，名将之村
　　Dapeng Fortress: Strategic Stronghold for Coastal Defense and Village of Famous Generals 198

07 吴阳：东海朝阳，状元故里
　　Wuyang: Hometown of the Top Successful Candidate of the Imperial Examination at the Highest Level, with the Sunrise Scene on the Eastern Sea 200

08 松口：南洋首站，客家侨乡
　　Songkou: First Stop to Southeast Asia and Hometown of Overseas Hakka People.....202

第八章 Chapter 8

八闽福地
Blessed Lands of Fujian Province

01 长汀：客家首府，红色山城
　　Changting: Principal City of the Hakka People and Revolution-Themed Mountainous City..206

02 和平：卵石城堡，进士之乡
　　Heping: A Castle of Pebbles and a Hometown of Successful Candidates of the Imperial Civil Examinations at the Highest Level..208

03 湖坑：土楼之乡，山居神话
　　Hukeng: A Hometown of *Tulou* and a Legend of Living in Mountains 210

04 塔下：南国之靖，太极水乡
　　Taxia: A Peaceful Land in Southern China and a Waterside Town Featuring Taiji (Supreme Ultimate) 212

05 芷溪：客家大宅，祠居合一
　　Zhixi: Mansions of the Hakka People Used as Temples and Residential Buildings 214

第一章
Chapter 1

江南水乡
Waterside Towns in the South of the Yangtze River

浙江
Zhejiang

乌镇：枕河而居，先锋江南
Wuzhen Town: Living by the River and a Pioneer in the South of the Yangtze River

上有天堂，下有苏杭。京杭大运河连接起两个"天堂"，中点便是乌镇。借水运之利，乌镇从宋代起便发展为商贸重镇，明清之际繁华愈炽，各类店铺作坊鳞次栉比。今天乌镇的游客仍可在作坊学着亲手染制一块蓝花布、制一支湖笔。富庶的乌镇人临水构屋，街巷遇水则以桥相连，形成了一幅水街相依、桥屋相连、家家面水、户户枕河的水墨长卷。遵循"修旧如旧"的原则，乌镇的江南古韵得以完美留存，恰如每个人的"梦里水乡"。乌镇，也被世界互联网大会选为永久会址，站到了信息时代的最前沿。江南多才子，乌镇的文化基因尤为浓厚，这里曾产生过六十四名进士、一百六十一位举人。近代则出过茅盾、木心等文化巨匠，茅盾故居和木心美术馆是到此不可错过的人文风景。乌镇戏剧节汇聚了来自世界各地的最优质的戏剧演出，或古典或先锋，精英荟萃、一票难求，已成为乌镇最耀眼的文化名片。

An ancient Chinese saying goes that "there is the Paradise above and Suzhou and Hangzhou below". The Beijing-Hangzhou Grand Canal connects the two "paradises", with Wuzhen Town as the midpoint. Availing itself of water transport, Wuzhen Town developed itself into a major trade town from the Song (960–1279) Dynasty. During the Ming (1368–1644) and Qing (1636–1912) dynasties, it ushered in greater prosperity, with rows of shops and workshops of all varieties. At present, visitors to Wuzhen Town can still learn to dye a piece of blue floral cloth and make a Huzhou writing brush in a workshop. The affluent people of Wuzhen Town have been building waterside houses. Streets are connected by bridges, forming an ink scroll with adjacent water, streets, connected bridges and houses, with each family facing the water or living by the river. Adhering to the principle of "repairing the old as old", the antique appeal of Wuzhen Town has been perfectly preserved, making it everyone's "dreamlike waterside towns". Wuzhen Town, also chosen as the permanent venue for World Internet Conference, stands at the forefront in the information age. There is a saying that talented scholars have abounded in the south of the Yangtze River. In particular, Wuzhen Town features a profound cultural flavor, having produced 64 *Jinshi* (successful candidates in the imperial civil examinations at the highest level) and 161 *Juren* (successful candidates in the imperial civil examinations at the provincial level). In the modern era, it witnessed the emergence of great cultural masters such as Mao Dun (1896–1981, a renowned Chinese novelist), and Mu Xin (1927-2011, a renowned Chinese writer and painter). Mao Dun's Former Residence and the Mu Xin Art Museum are humanistic scenic spots one should not miss. The Wuzhen Theatre Festival brings together the finest theatrical performances from the whole globe, including the classical and pioneering ones. With the assemblage of the elites, each ticket is fervently sought after. It has become the most dazzling cultural card of Wuzhen Town.

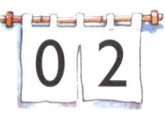

02 西塘：烟雨长廊，梦里西塘

Xitang: Dreamlike Xitang with Promenades Shrouded in the Misty Rain

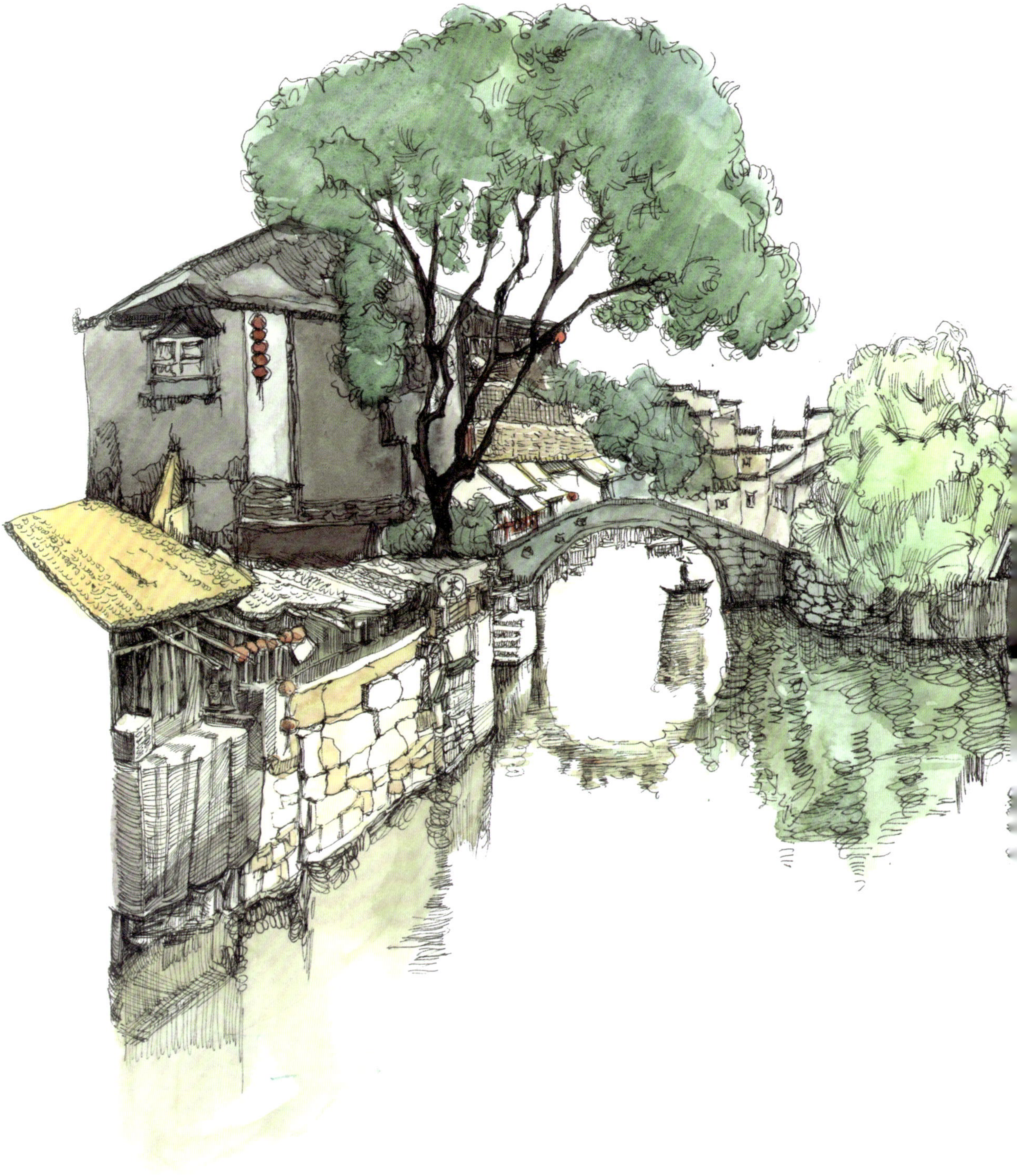

西塘，古称胥塘、斜塘。春秋吴越相争之时，伍子胥为屯兵引水凿河，这便是胥塘河。兵戈消歇，得天独厚的胥塘渐成鱼米之乡，明清时已发展为百业兴旺的繁华集镇。如今的西塘，还生活着大量原住民。弄堂里的馄饨担子，河塘里的鸬鹚捕鱼，手艺人的版画剪纸……水乡传统生活元素的留存使这座千年古镇生气流转、活色活现。连接河道与店铺的千米黑瓦廊棚是西塘最独特的风景，雨中漫步廊下，雨珠顺檐垂滴，看水面清圆，涟漪点点，烟雨江南，诗情满怀。入夜，著名的酒吧街流光溢彩，躁动着现代气息；清晨，小桥巷弄宁静如昔，氤氲着古朴清氛。

Xitang was known as Xutang and Xietang in ancient times. During the Spring and Autumn period (770 BC–476 BC) when the Wu and Yue states were fighting, Wu Zixu (559–484 BC, politician in the Wu State) ordered digging a canal to fetch water for his troops. It was known as the Xutang River. When the warfare subsided, Xutang, favored by nature, gradually became a town of abundance. By the Ming and Qing dynasties, it had developed into a prosperous market town with various booming trades. At present, a large number of indigenous people still live in Xitang. The wontons sold by peddlers in the alleyways, the cormorants fishing in the river ponds, the printmaking papercuts of the craftsmen... The survival of these traditional elements of life in the waterside town enables this millennium-old town to be brimming with vitality and prosperity. The black-tiled verandas connecting the riverways and the shopfronts, which stretch thousands of meters, are the most unique scenery in Xitang. Strolling under a veranda in the rain, you will see raindrops dripping down the eaves. Gazing at the clear and round water surface, you can admire the ripples amid a poetic feeling of the south of the Yangtze River shrouded in misty rain. At night, the famous bar street is full of brilliant lights and vibrant colors, revealing incessant pulses of modernity. In the morning, small bridges and lanes are as quiet as ever, with an antique and tranquil ambiance.

03 南浔：中西合璧，园林宅第
Nanxun: Garden-Like Mansions where the East Meets the West

在密如繁星的江南古镇中，南浔以中西合璧的建筑风格独树一帜。南浔位于江浙交界处，明清时便是蚕丝名镇，富商巨贾在此留下了众多清丽典雅的大宅园林。清末民初，敏锐的南浔丝商通过进出口贸易积聚了巨额财富，并将西方的建筑文化和礼节风俗带回了古镇。走进被誉为"江南第一宅"的张石铭旧居，人们惊讶地发现在古香古色粉墙黛瓦的大宅深处，竟还隐藏着一幢华丽的巴洛克风格的法式红砖建筑，洋楼一层便是铺着法式地板的宏丽舞厅。置身其间，百年前的衣香鬓影、舞步翩跹仿佛萦绕眼前。南浔素称"诗书之乡"，文杰辈出，百年前镇上的小学就开设了英语课，显示了南浔人超越时代的开阔视野。

In ancient towns scattered about like stars in the area south of the Yangtze River, Nanxun stands out for its unique blend of Chinese and Western architectural styles. Located in Huzhou, Zhejiang province, Nanxun was a famous silk town in the Ming and Qing dynasties, where wealthy and influential merchants left behind many beautiful and elegant garden-like mansions. In the late Qing Dynasty and early Republic of China, the Nanxun silk merchants amassed a huge fortune through import and export trade and brought back Western architectural culture and its manners and customs to the ancient town. In the Former Residence of Zhang Shiming (1871–1927), which is hailed as the "No.1 Mansion in the South of the Yangtze River", you will be surprised to find a magnificent French red brick building in Baroque style hidden in the depth of the ancient mansion with white walls and black tiles. Its first floor is a magnificent ballroom with French-style flooring. Standing inside, you seem to be gazing at a place with people finely dressed and taking elegant dance steps from one hundred years ago. Nanxun has been known as a "town of culture", with literary talents coming forth in large numbers. Since one hundred years ago, English classes have been offered in the town's primary schools, showing the Nanxun people's broad vision beyond the times.

04 石浦：山城渔港，海钓天堂
Shipu: Fishing Port and Marine Angling Paradise

石浦地处东海之滨，以"溪流入海处，山岩直逼海中"而得名。它是我国最早的海洋渔业发祥地之一，秦汉时即有先民在此耕海渔牧，唐宋时已成为远近闻名的繁华商埠，是"海上丝绸之路"的桥头堡之一。石浦古城沿山而筑，依山临海，正所谓"城在港上，山在城中"，它一头连着渔港、一头深藏在山间谷地，"居高控港"是这座军事重镇的海防利器，明代抗倭名将戚继光亦曾在此督战。水产丰富的石浦如今是全国渔业第一镇，也是海钓爱好者心中的天堂，每年在此举办的"国际海钓节"吸引着国内外游客纷至沓来，享受来自海洋的美好馈赠。

Located on the shores of the East China Sea, Shipu, literally meaning Rocky Shore, is named after a poetic line that "where the streams and rivers enter the oceans, the rocky outcrops stretch into the seas". It was one of the earliest birthplaces of marine fishing in China, with ancestors engaged in sea farming and ranching as early as the Qin (221–207 BC) and Han (202 BC–220 AD) dynasties. During the Tang (618–907) and Song dynasties, the city became a widely reputable trading port and a bridgehead of the Maritime Silk Road. Shipu Ancient Town is built along the mountains and beside the seas. As a saying goes, "the city is on the port while the mountains are in the city." With a fishing port at one end and a valley deep in the mountains at the other, its position of "standing high to control the port" was a great weapon of maritime defense for this strategic military town. It was here that Qi Jiguang (1528–1588), a famous general against Japanese pirates in the Ming Dynasty, supervised the battles. With its abundant aquatic products, Shipu is now the No.1 fishing town in China. It is a paradise for maritime angling enthusiasts. Every year, the International Sea Fishing Festival, which is held here, attracts tourists from home and abroad to enjoy wonderful gifts from the seas.

05 前童：清溪绕舍，诗礼儒乡
Qiantong: Clear Streams Around Houses in a Culturally Prosperous Town

前童始建于南宋末年，盛于明清，至今仍有千余间明清建筑存留完好，是浙东儒风最盛的古镇。前童山环水绕，整个村落是九宫八卦式"回"字布局，尤为令人称叹的是环绕在家家户户门前的八卦水系，童氏祖先依照易理引白溪水缘渠入村，清溪叮咚绕舍环流，正所谓"家家连流水小桥，户户通卵石曲径"。童氏家族耕读传家，童氏七世祖童伯礼曾两度礼聘明代大儒方孝孺来石镜精舍讲学，共同奠定了前童诗礼儒乡的基础。方孝孺还亲自参与设计了童氏宗祠，孕育了童氏的宗族精神。宗祠位于整个村落布局的中心，混合隋唐和明代的建筑风格，十分独特，值得一观。时光远去，但华美的雕窗、巍峨的马头墙和精巧的脊塑墙花，仍无言诉说着古镇昔日的繁盛。

Qiantong in Ninghai of Ningbo City was built in the late Southern Song Dynasty and flourished in the Ming and Qing dynasties. With over one thousand intact buildings from the Ming and Qing dynasties, it is the most culturally prosperous town in eastern Zhejiang. Qiantong is surrounded by mountains and rivers. The whole village features a nine-palace and eight-trigram layout. In particular, the most amazing aspect is the eight-trigram water system in front of every household. Ancestors of the Tong's Clan, following the principles in the *Book of Changes*, diverted water from the Baixi Stream to go through ditches and into the village. With the clear streams tinkling around the houses, it reminds of a saying that "Every house connects to flowing water under bridges. Each home links the meandering paths paved with pebbles." The Tong Clan has a time-honored clan lineage passed on by farming and reading. Tong Boli (1337–1395), the seventh ancestor of the Tong's Clan, twice invited Fang Xiaoru (1357–1402), a great Confucian of the Ming Dynasty, to come and lecture at the Shijing Jingshe (Stone Mirror Residence), laying the foundation for Qiantong to be a culturally prosperous town. Fang Xiaoru was also personally involved in the design of the Ancestral Hall of the Tong's Clan, which nurtured the spirit of the Tong's Clan. The ancestral hall is located in the center of the village's layout. As a unique mix of the architectural styles of the Sui (581–618), Tang (618–907), and Ming dynasties, it is worthy of a visit. As time passes by, the ornate carved windows, lofty horse-head walls, and elaborate ridge floral patterns are silent manifestations of the ancient town's former prosperity.

06 廿八都：百姓古塞，文化飞地
Nianbadu: Ancient Fortress and Cultural Enclave

唐末黄巢起兵南下时，曾在闽浙崇山峻岭间开辟了一条仙霞古道，成为后世兵家必争之地。随着海上丝绸之路的兴起，仙霞古道作为明清时期连接江浙闽的唯一陆上通路，又成为商旅要道。地处三省交界的廿八都作为古道上过往货物的头站，从屯兵之所变成明清盛极一时的繁华商埠，熙来攘往，商贾云集，富足热闹数百年之久。廿八都起于屯兵，兴于商贸，历代的残兵客商聚居于此，不同地域文化在此交汇碰撞、融合扬弃，形成了独一无二的"文化飞地"现象，小小一镇竟有十三种方言、一百四十二个姓氏。藏于深山、关隘拱立的独特地势，使这座千年古镇完美地躲过了战火纷扰，保留了大量明清建筑和民间艺术。今天许多传统手艺人依然在此生活，感受乡野之乐，传承历史记忆。

In the late period of the Tang Dynasty, when Huang Chao (820–884, leader of a peasant uprising) led his troops to march southward, he opened up the Xianxia Ancient Road among the towering mountains and precipitous ridges of Fujian and Zhejiang, which became a place of strategic importance for future generations of military strategists. With the rise of the Maritime Silk Road, Xianxia Ancient Road, as the only land route connecting Jiangsu, Zhejiang, and Fujian in the Ming and Qing dynasties, became a major commercial and tourist route again. Located at the junction of three provinces, Nianbadu was the first stop for goods passing through the ancient road. It was transformed from a place for stationed troops to a prosperous trading port in the Ming and Qing dynasties. With streams of merchants, it became rich and bustling for centuries. Founded for stationing troops, Nianbadu flourished in trade and commerce. With the remnant soldiers and merchants living here for generations, different regional cultures have met and collided with each other, with some elements absorbed and others discarded. It has created a unique "cultural enclave" phenomenon, with 13 dialects and 142 surnames in a tiny town. With unique terrain, hidden deep in the mountains and safeguarded by passes, this town escaped the turmoil of war to preserve many buildings and folk arts from the Ming and Qing dynasties. Many traditional craftsmen still live here today, enjoying the pleasure of the countryside and passing on their historical memories.

07 俞源：太极星象，文运昌盛
Yuyuan: Astrology of the Supreme Ultimate Indicates Cultural Prosperity

俞源俞姓最多，据《俞氏宗谱》记载，俞源村是明朝开国谋士刘伯温按天体星象布局而成，充分体现了"天人合一"的道家智慧。俞源四面环山，穿村而过的曲溪呈S形流向田野，勾勒出一个占地百亩的巨型太极图，并与周围的十一道山岗一起构成了黄道十二宫。八卦形排列的堂楼对应二十八星宿。村中水塘水井则对应北斗七星，称为"七星塘""七星井"。俞氏家族文运昌盛，明清两朝出过二百六十多名进士举人，据说正是因为俞氏宗祠坐落于七星"斗魁"之内，而"魁星"又称为文昌星。风水星象之说未必当真，但建于明代的俞氏宗祠气势恢宏、巧夺天工，非常值得一观。俞源现存宋元明清古建一千余间，其间雕刻精美绝伦，特别是建于康熙年间的声远堂有条百鱼梁，上有九条木雕鲤鱼会随着季节气候的变化改变颜色，甚为奇妙。

The people surnamed Yu account for the largest proportion of Yuyuan's population. According to the *Genealogy of the Yu Clan*, the village of Yuyuan was laid out according to the astrology by Liu Ji (1311–1375), the founding strategist of the Ming Dynasty. The layout fully embodies the Taoist wisdom of the "Unity of Heaven and Humanity". Yuyuan is surrounded by mountains on all sides. A curving stream runs in an S shape through the village and into the fields, outlining with the mountains a giant Taoist diagram of the *Taiji* (Supreme Ultimate) that covers an area of 6.67 hectares. Together with the 11 surrounding hillocks, it forms the 12 signs of the zodiac. The eight-trigram arrangement of the hall buildings corresponds to the 28 lunar mansions. The ponds and wells in the village, which correspond to the seven stars of the Big Dipper, are called the "Seven-Star Ponds" and "Seven-Star Wells". It is said that the Yu Clan was so culturally prosperous that over 260 successful candidates of the imperial civil examinations at the highest and provincial levels emerged during the Ming and Qing dynasties, and such cultural prosperity was due to the fact that the clan was located within the first to the fourth stars of the seven stars of the Great Dipper. These stars are also known as the Kui (Great Bear) Stars or the Wenchang (Cultural Prosperity) Stars. Although the Fengshui geomantic omen astrology may not be true, the Ancestral Hall of the Yu Clan, built in the Ming Dynasty, is a magnificent and ingenious work of art, which is well worth a visit. Yuyuan is home to over 1,000 ancient buildings from the Song, Yuan, Ming and Qing dynasties, which are beautifully carved. In particular, the Shengyuan Hall, built during Emperor Kangxi's reign (1662–1722), has a beam carved with fish, among which are nine carved wooden carps with changeable colors according to the seasons and climates. It is a wonderful sight.

08 郭洞：风水福地，长寿之乡
Guodong: Land of Fengshui Geomantic Omen and Longevity

郭洞藏于浙江武义山间，有"江南第一风水村"的美誉。此地三面青山环抱，双溪汇注，北面留一平地，正合堪舆学"狮象把门"之妙。郭洞先祖可追溯至宋朝宰相何执中，元代何氏子孙仿照道家《内经图》布局营造了整个村落。村头砌城墙形成水口，建回龙桥聚气藏风，环村植林，规划民居并巧设七星井，形成"山环如郭，幽邃如洞"的佳境，故名郭洞。何氏家族在此绵延不息，世代书香，人才辈出。郭洞还是著名的长寿之乡，如今村中生活着几十位高寿长者，这多半得益于郭洞绝佳的生态环境。村东龙山覆盖着苍莽的原始森林，翠嶂千重，可谓天然氧吧。山中古树参天、名木极多，其中最珍贵的当数恐龙时代就已存在的南方红豆杉了。

Hidden in the mountains of Wuyi in Zhejiang, Guodong is known as the "No.1 Fengshui geomantic omen village in the south of the Yangtze River". The land is surrounded by green hills on three sides, with two streams converging, leaving a flat area on the north. It is a perfect match for the "gate guarding by the lion and the elephant" in terms of geomancy. Guodong's ancestors can be traced back to Prime Minister He Zhizhong in the Song Dynasty. The entire village was created by He's descendants in the Yuan Dynasty (1271–1368), following the layout of the Taoist *Inner Classic*. At the village's entrance, a wall was built to form a water outlet, while the Huilong (Dragon-Returning) Bridge was built to gather air and hide the wind. Forests were planted around the village. Dwellings were planned and seven-star wells were set up, creating a beautiful scenery of "having the mountains as its outer walls and possessing a profound and unfathomable meaning like that of a cave," hence the name Guodong, literally meaning "outer wall" and "cave". The He Clan has been living here for generations, passing the clan lineage with scholarly fame and emerging talents. Guodong is also famous for being a land of longevity, with dozens of long-lived elderly people living in the village, mostly thanks to Guodong's excellent ecological environment. To the east of the village is the Longshan (Dragon) Mountain, which is vast with overlapping green peaks. It can be hailed as a natural oxygen bar. The mountains abound in towering ancient trees and famous trees, the most precious of which is the Taxus Chinensis (Chinese yew), which has existed since the times of dinosaurs.

江苏
Jiangsu

周庄：方圆双桥，水乡之最
Zhouzhuang: Waterside Town with Twin Bridges and Enchantiing Scenery

陈逸飞的双桥油画、张艺谋的水乡电影，使周庄成为最早被"发现"的江南古镇。吴冠中曾言"黄山集中国山川之美，周庄集中国水乡之美"，这座有九百余年历史的苏州小镇，古风犹存、容颜依旧，可以满足人们对古韵江南的所有想象。"井"字形河道流贯周庄，沿河八条长街房檐相接粉墙黛瓦，河中碧水悠悠摇橹咿呀，十四座建于元明清各朝的古石桥造型各异身姿曼妙。钥匙桥一方一圆错落有致，富安桥楼桥合璧相映成趣。相传周庄兴自江南巨富沈万三，至今万三蹄、万三糕仍是周庄的特色佳肴。沈氏后人建于清代的沈厅，恢宏精美，是江南民宅建筑的典范。建于明代的大宅张厅气派非凡，后院设有"私家码头"，正所谓"轿从门前进，船在家中过"，意趣盎然，极富特色。

The oil painting of the Twin Bridges (Key Bridges) by Chen Yifei (1946–2005, a Chinese painter) and the films of waterside towns by Zhang Yimou (1950–, a Chinese director) made Zhouzhuang one of the first ancient towns in the south of the Yangtze River to be "discovered". Wu Guanzhong (1919–2010, a Chinese painter) once said, "Mount Huangshan integrates the beauty of China's mountains and rivers, while Zhouzhuang gathers the beauty of China's water towns." Located in Suzhou, this small town features a history of over 900 years. Having preserved its ancient style and past look, it can satisfy all the imaginations for the antique appeal of the south of the Yangtze River. The groined river runs through Zhouzhuang. On eight long streets along the river, the eaves of the houses see connected white walls and black tiles. Squeaking oars are heard from the blue, languid river. Fourteen ancient stone bridges built in the Yuan, Ming, and Qing dynasties, in their different shapes and sizes, reveal their lithe and graceful gestures. The Key Bridges, with a square and a round bridge, features attractive disorder. The Fu'an Bridge and its bridge buildings form a delightful contrast with each other. According to legend, Zhouzhuang's prosperity began in the lifetime of Shen Wansan (1306–1394, an ancient Chinese merchant), a wealthy man from the south of the Yangtze River. To this day, Wansan Pig's Trotter and Wansan Pastry are still among the specialties of Zhouzhuang. Built by the descendants of the Shen Family in the Qing Dynasty, the Shen Hall is magnificent and exquisite, being an example of residential buildings in the south of the Yangtze River. Built in the Ming Dynasty, the mansion, known as Zhang Hall, features an imposing manner, with a "private dock" in the back yard echoing the notion that "sedan chairs go in from the front gate while boats pass through the mansion", making it full of interest, charm, and characteristics.

10 同里：繁华富土，醇正水乡
Tongli: Prosperous and Intoxicatingly Pure Waterside Town

同里地处苏州鱼米之乡，六千年前已有人烟，秦成集市，因其富庶故称"富土"。唐初因名太侈改为"铜里"；宋代将旧名"富土"两字相迭，拆字为"同里"，此后四朝便有了繁华日盛的吴中重镇"同里"。同里共分七岛，镶嵌于五湖之中，由四十九座古桥连为一体，家家临河、户户摇橹。因过去与外界只通舟楫，鲜受兵祸，时光在此留驻，明清风貌未改，古建数量极多。"品"字型排列的三座明清古桥——太平、吉利、长庆，寓意美好，同里人"走三桥"祈福的习俗延续至今。退思园小巧玲珑如浮水上，移步换景千变万化，古人构园之妙令人称叹。古老的南园茶社陈设如昨，点一盏清茗，临河遥想，仿佛回到了百年前柳亚子、陈去病在此商讨南社成立的良夜。

Tongli is located in Suzhou, which is hailed as a land of abundance. Tracing back to its earliest inhabitation 6,000 years ago, it became a marketplace in the Qin Dynasty (221–207 BC). It has been known as Futu (rich land) because of its affluence. In the early Tang Dynasty (618–907), its name, for being too lavish, was changed to "Tongli". In the Song Dynasty, it was also known as "Tongli" (with different Chinese characters from the first Tongli.) From then on, there had been "Tongli" as an increasingly prosperous town and as a town of military significance in the land of Wu. Tongli is divided into seven islands, with all of them set in the middle of five lakes. They are connected by forty-nine ancient bridges, with every family facing the river and every house sculling. In the past, only boats were used to communicate with the outside world, causing few military disasters. With time seeming to stop here, it has retained its landscape of the Ming and Qing dynasties, with a great multitude of ancient buildings. The three ancient bridges of the Ming and Qing dynasties, including the Taiping (Great Peace), Jili (Auspice), and Changqing (Lasting Celebration) Bridges, are arranged in the shape of a triangle and have a good meaning. The custom of "walking on the three bridges" to pray for good fortune continues to this day. The Tuisi (Retreat and Reflection) Garden is so exquisite and fine that it seems to be floating on the water. When seeing a different view with each step forward, you cannot help admiring the gardening wonders of the ancients. The time-honored Nanyuan (South Garden) Tea House is furnished as it was in the past. You can order a cup of clear tea and ponder by the river as if you have returned to the good night when Liu Yazi (1886–1958, a Chinese politician and poet) and Chen Qubing (1874–1933, a Chinese social activist and poet) discussed the establishment of the South Society (a revolutionary literature group) here one hundred years ago.

甪直：五湖六泽，三步两桥
Luzhi: Five Lakes, Six Marshes, and Two Bridges within Three Steps

　　甪直位于苏州城东，镇域有澄湖等五湖环抱，距今已有两千五百年历史。甪直原名甫里，后因镇东有直港，通向吴淞江等六处河道，水流形似"甪"字，故更名"甪直"。茅以升称甪直为桥梁博物馆，在方圆一千米的古镇内，建有宋元明清四朝石拱桥七十二座，现存四十一座。古桥之密举世无双，就连威尼斯也甘拜下风。到甪直必访千年名刹保圣寺，它是"南朝四百八十寺"历经数代风雨沧桑后的遗珠。寺中仅存的九座泥塑罗汉乃唐代"塑圣"杨惠之的真迹，千年后神韵不失，令人叹为观止。水乡之韵在水。坐一坐摇橹船，船娘梳髻髻头、着拼接衫，"青莲仙子藕荷裳"，是甪直独有的风情；尝一尝水八仙宴，茭白胜雪，红菱鲜嫩，"软温新剥鸡头肉"，是江南水灵灵的"秀色可餐"。

　　Located in the east of Suzhou City, Luzhi embraces five lakes, including Chenghu Lake. With a history of 2,500 years, it was originally named Fuli. Luzhi was later used as its name because in the east of the town is the Zhigang Habor whose water runs in a shape of a Chinese character pronounced "Lu" to six river channels, including the Wusong River and others. Mao Yisheng (1896–1989, a Chinese structural engineer) called Luzhi "a museum of bridges". Within the one-kilometer radius of the ancient town, 72 stone arch bridges were built during the Song, Yuan, Ming, and Qing dynasties, 41 of which have been preserved. Its ancient bridges are so densely scattered that they are unparalleled in the world; even Venice can't match. A must-see destination in Luzhi is the millennium-old Baosheng Temple, a relic of the "480 temples of the Southern Dynasty" that have survived the vicissitudes of several generations. The nine remaining clay sculptures of Arhats in the temple are the authentic works of Yang Huizhi (around the eighth century), hailed as the saint of sculpture in the Tang Dynasty. They have retained their divine appeal after millennia. The appeal of the waterside towns lies in the water. Sitting on a rowed boat, you can admire boat ladies with their topknots and patchwork shirts. "Like a green lotus fairy, she wears the dress with the patterns of lotus roots and leaves." This depicts the unique style of Luzhi. You can also have a feast of the Eight Immortal Aquatic Products, where you can have a bite of the wild rice shoots whiter than snow and of the fresh and tender red caltrop. "They are soft and warm like freshly processed chicken." It is an edible portion of the fresh and beautiful landscape unique to the area south of the Yangtze River.

12 木渎：园林古镇，秀冠江南
Mudu: Ancient Town of Gardens, Being the Best of the South of the Yangtze River

相传春秋末年，吴王夫差为取悦美人西施在灵岩山顶建馆娃宫，木材源源而至，竟堵塞了山下的河流，"积木塞渎"，苏州西郊山麓的这个小镇便由此得名。木渎繁盛千载，商贾辐辏，明清时期有园林私宅三十余处，既秉承了苏州园林的精致幽深，又添空旷高远之致。在清代徐扬所绘《姑苏繁华图》中，木渎占了一半篇幅。康熙三次南巡、乾隆六下江南，都曾在此停驻。徐士元的虹饮山房，是乾隆来木渎必游之地。若论园林之胜、文蕴之深，严家花园又比这"民间行宫"更胜一筹，它的第一代主人是清代名士沈德潜，后转给诗人钱端溪，最后被木渎首富严国馨买下，由建筑大师姚承祖修葺一新，布局精妙无匹，遂成园林翘楚。古镇西北的灵岩山以奇石险峰闻名于世，有"灵岩秀绝冠江南"之美誉。与之遥遥相对的天平山则是中国四大赏红胜地之一，金秋时节红枫清泉，美不胜收。

According to legend, at the end of the Spring and Autumn period (770 BC–476 BC), King Fuchai (r. 495–473 BC) of the Wu state built the Guanwa Palace at the top of Lingyan Mountain to please his concubine Xishi (503-473 BC, famous Chinese beauty). The timbers came in such a steady stream that they blocked the river at the foot of the mountain, hence the saying that "accumulated timbers (Mu) blocked a river (Du)". This is the source of the name of this town at the foot of the mountains on the western outskirts of Suzhou. Mudu has been prosperous for millennia, with bustling merchants' carts and horses. During the Ming and Qing dynasties, there were more than 30 private gardens and mansions in Mudu, which were not only as refined and secluded as Suzhou gardens but also imbued with the elegance of being open and lofty. In the painting titled *A Painting of the Prosperous Gusu* by Xu Yang (around the 18th century) in the Qing Dynasty, half of the painting space is taken up by scenes of Mudu. Emperor Kangxi (1661–1722) made three southern tours and Emperor Qianlong (1736–1796) made six trips to the south of the Yangtze River, all stopping here. The Hongyin (Rainbow Drinking) Mountain Manor of Xu Shiyuan (around the 18th century) was a must-see destination for Emperor Qianlong (1736–1796) whenever he came to Mudu. The Yan Family Garden is even better than the "folk temporary imperial residence" in terms of the beauty of the gardens and the profoundness of the cultural connotations. The first owner was Shen Deqian (1673–1769), a famous scholar of the Qing Dynasty, who later passed it on to the poet Qian Duanxi (around the 19th century), and it was finally bought by Yan Guoxin (?–1993), the richest man in Mudu. Renovated by master architect Yao Chengzu (1866–1938, Chinese architect), the garden features an exceptionally exquisite layout, enabling it to become the leading garden. The Lingyan Mountain in the northwest of the town is famous for its grotesque rocks and perilous peaks, enjoying the reputation that "Lingyan is the most beautiful mountain in the south of the Yangtze River". On its distant opposite is the Tianping (Heavenly Peace) Mountain, one of the four major destinations for viewing red maples in China, where the red maples and clear springs present an overwhelming visual feast in the golden autumn.

锦溪：碧荷长堤，莲池古桥
Jinxi: Long Embankments Lined by Green Lotus Leaves; Ancient Bridges amid Lotus Ponds

锦溪地处昆山南郊淀山湖畔，吴越春秋之时已成集镇，历史悠久，诗文不绝。它名气虽不如近邻周庄，丰韵天成的湖景却足以惊艳众生，沈从文喻锦溪为"睡梦中的少女"，刘海粟赞它为"水乡之最"。穿过窄街小巷，至古镇东首豁然开朗，眼前是一碧万顷、烟波浩渺的湖水，古莲长堤如长虹卧波，将菱塘湾和五保湖分隔开来。堤上数百米的朱红廊桥飞檐翘角倒映水中，夏日桥下莲叶接天风荷无边，恍若仙境。长堤左首不远处有一个芦草萋萋的"独圩墩"，那便是著名的陈妃水冢。史载宋孝宗将宠妃陈妃水葬于她生前极爱之地，并改地名为"陈墓"。长堤右首是孝宗为超度陈妃所建的莲池禅院，被誉为湖光霞影中的"水乡佛国"。锦溪还被称为"中国民间博物馆之乡"，金石、紫砂、奇石、根雕等各类藏品荟萃于此，其中最值得重视的是古砖瓦博物馆，那秦砖汉瓦见证了历史沧桑，也记载了锦溪繁盛数百年的砖瓦文化。

Located on the shores of Dianshan Lake in the southern suburbs of Kunshan, Jinxi features a time-honored history with its establishment as a market town during the Spring and Autumn period (770–476 BC) and its literature pieces passed down generation after generation. Although it is not as famous as its neighboring Zhouzhuang, its naturally appealing lake landscape is stunning enough to make Shen Congwen (1902–1988, a Chinese novelist) describe Jinxi as a "sleeping maiden" and Liu Haisu (1896–1994, a Chinese painter and fine arts educator) praise it as "the best of the waterside towns". After passing through the narrow streets and alleys, you will reach the east end of the town which opens up to a vast lake, with the ancient lotus embankment lying like a rainbow, separating Lingtang (Water Caltrop Pond) Bay and Wubao (Five-Protection) Lake. The vermillion corridor bridge with a length of hundreds of meters on the embankment sees its overhanging eaves and cornices reflected in the water. In summer, the vast stretches of lotus leaves under the bridge are like a fairyland. A short distance to the left of the long embankment is the famous Duweidun (Single Dike Mound) surrounded by lush reeds; it is the famous waterside graveyard of Concubine Chen. According to historical records, in the Song Dynasty (960–1279), Emperor Xiaozong (r. 1162–1194) buried his favorite Concubine Chen in the place she loved dearly during her lifetime, with the place renamed "Chenmu" ("Chen's Grave"). At the right end of the long embankment is the Lianchi (Lotus Pond) Zen Monastery, built by Emperor Xiaozong to bring peace to Concubine Chen's soul. It has been renowned as a "Buddhist kingdom in a waterside town" amid the landscape of the lake and the twilight. Jinxi is also known as the "town of Chinese folk museums", gathering various collections of inscribed bronzes and stone tablets, red stonewares, grotesque stones, root carvings, and others. The most important one is the Guzhuanwa (Ancient Brick and Tile) Museum, where the bricks and tiles from the Qin and Han dynasties bear witness to the vicissitudes of history and record the centuries-old brick and tile culture that flourished in Jinxi.

14 千灯：炎武故里，昆腔绕梁
Qiandeng: Hometown of Yanwu and the Land with Reverberating Music of Kun Opera

闻"千灯"之名，眼前已现桨声灯影的诗情画意，但实际上"千灯"是"千墩"的谐音，名出吴越争霸时的一千座烽火台。这座美丽千年的昆山古镇，是著名爱国主义思想家顾炎武的家乡，访其故居，先生那句"天下兴亡，匹夫有责"的铿锵之语在心头激荡。千灯还是"百戏之祖"昆曲的发源地，元末明初戏曲家顾坚世居于此。走进这位昆曲鼻祖的纪念馆，在婉转端丽的水磨腔中，中国戏曲发展史一一呈现。始建于南朝的秦峰塔是古镇地标，云雾中时隐时现，清风中梵铃声动，众妙难言。古镇桥多，"三桥邀月"是千灯名景，三座古桥联袂而筑，分呈宋、明、清三朝特色，流水东逝，历史于此处交汇。

Hearing the name of Qiandeng (one thousand lanterns), you seem to be seeing the picturesque appeal amid the squeaking oars and the shining lanterns. However, in fact, Qiandeng is a homonym for Qiandun (one thousand mounds), a name that originated from one thousand beacon towers from the time of rivalry between the Wu and Yue states for hegemony in the Spring and Autumn period (770–476 BC). Kunshan Ancient Town, which has been a land of great beauty for millennia, is the hometown of Gu Yanwu (1613–1682), a famous patriotic thinker. Any visitor to his hometown will feel the mental reverberation of his sonorous saying that "one has a duty towards the rises and falls of one's motherland." Qiandeng is also the birthplace of Kun Opera hailed as the "ancestor of all Chinese operas". The family of Gu Jian (around 1368), an opera master from the late Yuan and early Ming dynasties, lived here for generations. After entering the memorial hall of this patriarch of the Kun Opera, you will see the unfolding of the developmental history of the Chinese opera amid the suave, neat, and beautiful melodies of the Kun Opera. The Qinfeng Pagoda, built in the Southern Dynasty (420–589), is a landmark of the ancient town. As it looms in the clouds and mist, you will hear the Buddhist bells ringing in the clear breeze and feel indescribable wonders. This ancient town abounds in bridges. The spot of "Three Bridges Inviting the Moon" is a famous sight. The three ancient bridges were built adjacent to each other, showing the characteristics of the Song, Ming, and Qing dynasties. As the water flows eastwards, different branches of history intersect here.

15 惠山：二泉映月，泥人纳福
Huishan: Spring Reflecting the Moon and Clay Figurines Bringing Fortune

无锡市惠山古镇南邻万顷太湖，因境内有惠山而得名。京杭大运河留经古镇腹地，水陆两便之地利使惠山在明代便成为商贸中心，清中叶成为全国"四大米市"之一。自唐宋起，名门望族便在惠山兴建祠堂，明清更盛。古镇现存自唐以降历代祠堂一百一十八处，古雅清隽的碑刻和精妙绝伦的建筑令人叹为观止，祠堂文化留存之完整举世瞩目。始建于南北朝的千年名刹惠山寺留下了无数帝王将相、文人雅士的足迹，唐代茶圣陆羽到此品泉，称惠山石泉为"天下第二泉"，从此石泉更名"二泉"，名动天下。"瞎子阿炳"创作于此的二胡名曲《二泉映月》，如泣如诉、闻之心碎，为第二泉添了几许凄美。寺畔的寄畅园巧借天然、构园精妙，乾隆南巡时爱其景致，遂在帝都清漪园仿此建造了谐趣园。古镇还有一绝是以"大阿福"为代表作的惠山泥人，其造型饱满、色彩绚丽，惟妙惟肖、雅俗共赏，是民间艺术中的珍品。

Huishan Ancient Town, which is located to the north of Taihu Lake in Wuxi City, is named after the Huishan Mountain in its territory. The Beijing-Hangzhou Grand Canal, which sits astride Wuxi, made Huishan a center of trade and commerce in the Ming Dynasty. In the mid-Qing Dynasty, it became one of the "Four Great Rice Markets" of China. Since the Tang and Song dynasties, famous families had built ancestral halls in Huishan; it was a practice of greater prosperity in the Ming and Qing dynasties. There are now 118 ancestral halls from the Tang Dynasty onwards in the ancient town. The antique and elegant inscriptions and exquisite buildings have been acclaimed as the peak of perfection. The integrity of the ancestral hall culture is remarkable throughout the world. Built in the Northern and Southern dynasties (386–589), the millennium-old Huishan Temple has left behind the marks of numerous kings and generals, literati, and scholars. In the Tang Dynasty, Lu Yu (733–804), the sage of tea, came here to taste the spring water and called the Huishan stone spring the "Second Spring Under Heaven". From then on, Shiquan was renamed Erquan (the second spring), with its reputation spread across the world. The famous *Erhu* song *Erquan Yingyue* (The Moon Reflected on the Erquan Spring) was composed here by the blind artist A Bing (1893–1950, a renowned Chinese musician). It is mournful and heartbreaking, adding to the sad and beautiful ambiance of the second spring. Built next to the temple, the Jichang Garden features clever borrowing of natural elements and exquisite gardening composition techniques. Emperor Qianlong (1736–1796) was so fond of its scenery during his southern inspection tour that he built the Xiequ (Harmonious Charms) Garden in Qingyi (Clear Ripples) Garden in the imperial capital as an imitation of the Jichang Garden. Another exceptional item in the town is the Huishan clay figurines represented by *Da'afu* (fortunate chubby children). Having plumb shapes and bright colors, they are true to life and appealing to all tastes, enabling them to be treasures of folk art.

洞庭东山：碧螺春醉，洞庭橘红
Dongting Dongshan: Intoxicating Biluochun Green Tea and Red Tangerines of Dongting

　　苏州东山古镇是太湖中最大的一个陆连岛，因其在太湖洞山与庭山以东而得名。费孝通誉东山为"天堂中的天堂"，此地不仅风光殊胜，且物产极为丰饶。来到东山，春日定要品正宗的碧螺春茶，嫩香盈抱；秋日必要尝爽口的洞庭红橘，唇齿留香。还有白沙枇杷、太湖三白和莼菜等也是不可错过的东山特产。

　　古镇万余年前已有人烟，明清时期人文昌盛，留下众多古迹胜景，而今依旧掩映于湖光山色间。太湖之滨的启园是江南少有的山麓湖滨园林，园中既有藏山纳湖的万千气象，又不失苏式园林的精致玲珑。富丽恢弘的春在楼被誉为"江南第一楼"，因处处有精致繁复的雕花，集砖雕、木雕、金雕、石雕、壁画、匾额为一体，也被称为雕花大楼。地处清幽的千年古刹紫金庵里，藏着十六尊惟妙惟肖的泥塑彩绘罗汉像，相传是南宋泥塑圣手雷潮夫妇之作。

　　Suzhou's Dongshan Ancient Town, which is the largest land-tied island in Taihu Lake, is named after its location east of Dongshan and Tingshan mountains in Taihu Lake. Fei Xiaotong (1910–2005, a Chinese sociologist) described Dongshan as "the paradise of paradises". It is a place not only of exceptional beauty but also of great abundance. When you come to Dongshan, you must taste the authentic Biluochun green tea in spring, which is full of tenderness and fragrance, and the crisp Dongting red tangerines in autumn, which leaves a fragrant taste on your lips and teeth. Also not to be missed are the loquat from Baisha, the three white food ingredients from Taihu Lake, the water shield, and other specialties of Dongshan.

　　The town was inhabited over 10,000 years ago. During the Ming and Qing dynasties, the people and their culture flourished, leaving behind many monuments and scenic spots, which are still looming between the lake and the mountains at present. The Qiyuan Garden on the shores of Taihu Lake is one of the few lakeside gardens in the south of the Yangtze River. It features the grandeur of hiding mountains and lakes within the garden and the exquisiteness of a Suzhou-style garden. The magnificent Chunzai (Existent Spring) Building is hailed as the "First Building in the South of the Yangtze River". It has also been known as the Carved Building because of the exquisite and intricate carvings everywhere, integrating brick carving, wood carving, gold carving, stone carving, frescoes, and plaques. Zijin (Purple Gold) Nunnery, a millennium-old temple in a secluded and tranquil location, houses sixteen vivid clay statues of Arhats, which are said to be the works of Lei Chao and his wife, the sage clay sculptors of the Southern Song Dynasty.

震泽：吴头越尾，蚕丝之乡
Zhenze: Hometown of Silkworms at the Junction of the Wu and Yue States

震泽是苏州又一处千年古镇，因北临太湖，便借用了太湖诗意的别名"震泽"。古镇地处春秋时期吴越交界处，故有"吴头越尾"之称。京杭大运河穿镇而过，给这里带来了数百年的滚滚财源。震泽是四海闻名的蚕丝之乡，丝绸文化传承至今，游人到此可亲身体验一下采桑养蚕之乐。晚清时期震泽以丝市和米市著称，宝塔街上店铺商行林立、商贾辐辏，留下了不少精美古建，其中尤以师俭堂为最佳。师俭堂三面临水，占地两千五百平方米，是江南迄今保存完整的最大古民宅。它集河埠、行栈、商铺、街道、厅堂、内宅、花园、下房于一体，反映了晚清工商绅士坐行经商的时代特点。其雕饰之精美，可媲美洞庭东山的春在楼。师俭堂与古镇地标慈云塔遥相呼应。这座楼阁宝塔历经数百年风霜依旧巍峨挺秀，风吹梵铃、佛音清远。建于康乾盛世的禹迹桥与慈云塔相映成趣，夕阳中登塔远眺，湖光中拱桥塔影、云霞千里，如临仙境，是震泽独有的美景。

Zhenze is another millennium-old town in Suzhou. With the Taihu Lake to its north, it is named Zhenze (Shaking Marsh), borrowing the poetic nickname of the Taihu Lake. Located at the junction of the Wu and Yue states during the Spring and Autumn period (770 BC–476 BC), it is therefore known as the "the Head of the Wu State and the Tail of the Yue State". The Beijing-Hangzhou Grand Canal flows through the town, bringing unending wealth to the area for centuries. Zhenze is the globally renowned hometown of silkworms, with its silk culture passed down generation after generation. Visitors can experience the joy of picking mulberry leaves and raising silkworms here. During the late Qing Dynasty, Zhenze was famous for its silk and rice markets. Numerous shops and merchants on the Baota (Precious Pogoda) Street have left behind many exquisite old buildings, among which the Shijian Hall is the best. Facing the water on three sides and covering an area of 2,500 square meters, Shijian Hall is the largest well-preserved ancient residential building in the south of the Yangtze River. Incorporating the river dock, inn, shop, street, hall, inner house, garden, and servants' quarters, it has reflected the characteristics of the era when industrial and commercial figures lived and did business in the late Qing Dynasty. Its exquisite carving is comparable to that of the Chunzai (Spring's Presence) Building in the Dongshan Mountain of Dongting. The Shijian Hall echoes the Ciyun (Compassionate Cloud) Pagoda at a distance, which is a landmark of the ancient town. The pagoda, which has survived centuries of hardships, is still standing tall and beautiful, with the wind blowing the Buddhist bells and the clear Buddhist sounds reaching far and wide. Built during the booming and golden age of the Qing Dynasty - from Emperor Kangxi to Emperor Qianlong, the Yuji Bridge and the Ciyun Pagoda complement each other. In the setting sun, one ascends the pagoda, looks into the distance, and sees the shadow of the arch bridge and the pagoda under the vast stretches of the rose-tinted clouds, feeling as if in a fairyland. It is a unique scenic sight in Zhenze.

盛泽：丝绸之都，衣被天下
Shengze: Silk Capital Benefiting the World

　　苏州盛泽古镇是著名的丝绸之都，明清时期就以"日出万绸，衣被天下"而闻名于世。盛泽丝绸自明清时就远销海内外，而今声誉更隆，行销世界各国。古镇现存数座宏大华丽的会馆、庄面，见证了数百年间丝绸贸易的繁盛。织绸技艺在这里薪火相传，如今的盛泽既保有传承千年的手工操作，也拥有最现代的生产设备，堪称一座鲜活的丝绸博物馆。走进清代丝商公建的先蚕祠，拱门上书"织云""绣锦"，是对织绸工艺的诗意赞美；踏上始建于康熙朝的白龙桥，桥上所镌"风送万机声，晴翻千尺浪"，是对丝绸水乡的唯美写照。

Shengze Ancient Town in Suzhou is a famous silk capital, with its reputation for "producing over ten thousand bolts of silk to benefit the world" in the Ming and Qing dynasties. Shengze's silk has been sold in China and abroad since the Ming and Qing dynasties. At present, its reputation has grown greater with its silk being sold to countries all over the world. Several magnificent guilds and manors survive in the ancient town, bearing witness to the prosperity of the silk trade over the centuries. The art of silk weaving has been passed down for generations here. At present, Shengze is a living museum of silk with its millennia-old handwork and most modern production facilities. Walking into the Ancestral Silkworm Hall built by the silk merchants in the Qing Dynasty, you can see the memorial arch with the inscriptions of "Embroidered Clouds" and "Embroidered Brocade", which are poetic tributes to the craft of silk weaving. Stepping onto the Bailong (White Dragon) Bridge built during Emperor Kangxi's reign, you can see the couplets on the bridge, which read "amid the wind, the sounds of ten thousand looms spread; Even in the sunlight, one thousand feet of waves are heaved." It is a beautiful depiction of a waterside town of silk.

19 溱潼：水乡明珠，青砖绝响
Qintong: Pearl among Waterside Towns with Exceptional Brickwork

泰州溱潼古镇四面环水，长江、淮河、黄海在此交汇，西邻京杭大运河，是物产丰饶的鱼米之乡，也曾是商贸往来的重镇。溱潼现存古建六万多平米，其中多是仕宦商贾留下的精致宅第。与苏南的粉墙黛瓦不同，苏中建筑风格以青砖灰瓦、磨檐博山为主体。不论大宅小户，皆饰有精美无双的砖雕，这得益于当年溱潼兴盛的砖窑文化。溱湖底的淤泥黏密如胶，是烧砖最好的原料，百年前这里的富户家家取泥烧砖，制成的砖"色如绿豆青，声如小鼓响"，在北京故宫、上海城隍庙等著名建筑中都能看到溱砖的"双斧"标志。有智慧的溱潼人还以青砖竖着铺路，不以砂浆勾缝，遇人行走青砖撞击如金石之声，称为"响砖"，具有天然的防盗效果。如今砖窑已成历史，溱潼却仍以古朴清雅的风貌和传承千年的文化底蕴吸引着八方来客。若恰好赶上了溱潼会船节，溱湖中千帆竞发、兴风踏浪，游人又可大饱眼福。

Qintong Ancient Town in Taizhou is surrounded by water on all sides, where the Yangtze River, the Huaihe River, and the Yellow Sea meet. Adjacent to the Beijing-Hangzhou Grand Canal to its west, it is a town of abundance and was once a major town of trade and commerce. More than 60,000 square meters of ancient buildings have been preserved in Qintong, most of which are exquisite mansions left behind by officials and merchants. Unlike the white walls and black tiles of southern Suzhou, the architectural style of central Suzhou is dominated by green bricks, grey tiles, polished eaves, and gabled roofs. No matter how large or small, all residential buildings are decorated with exquisite brick carvings, thanks to the flourishing brick kiln culture in Qintong. The mud at the bottom of the Zhenhu Lake, which is as sticky as glue, is the best raw material for burning bricks. One hundred years ago, wealthy families fetched the mud to make bricks, which are "as green as mung beans, sounding like snare drums." The "Double Axe" sign of Qintong's bricks can be seen in the Forbidden City in Beijing, the Town God's Temple of Shanghai, and other famous buildings. The wise Qintong people also pave the roads with vertical bricks, using no mortar joints. Stepping on the bricks produce sounds of hitting bronzes and stone tablets, earning the name of "loud bricks" and producing a natural anti-theft effect. At present, the brick kilns were something in the past, but Qintong still features a quaint and elegant landscape and a millennium-old cultural heritage to attract visitors from all directions. If you are in time for the Qintong Boat Festival, you will be able to have a visual feast with thousands of sails braving waves on the Zhenhu Lake.

20 朱家角：沪上名镇，船拳之乡
Zhujiajiao: Famous Town in Shanghai and Hometown for Boat Boxing

淀山湖滨、九峰北麓，一座千年小镇如水墨折扇铺展于湖光山色间，这便是朱家角。朱家角地处江浙沪交界处，槽港河穿镇而过，水路四通八达，是沪区通往京杭大运河的门户。五千年前此处已有人烟，宋元时形成集镇，明清时成为长三角商贸重镇，漕船云集、烟火千家。民国时近代工商业蓬勃发展，有"上海威尼斯"之称。曾令水盗、倭寇闻风丧胆的江南船拳即发源于此，百年前这里几乎家家练拳，至今武林薪火相传。船拳综合三国时吴军水战之法和少林寺梅花桩等武术而自成一派，能在船头方寸之间辗转腾挪制敌取胜，是漕民护船保家的绝技。每年端午行街之时，放生桥下的船拳表演总能赢得震天喝彩。放生桥建于明代，人称"沪上第一桥"，是江南最大的五孔大石桥。站于桥顶观摇快船赛，但见河中百舸争流、拨桨如飞，金鼓阗沸、好不热闹！

On the shores of the Dianshan Lake and at the northern foot of the Jiufeng Peak, a millennium-old town spreads out like an ink folding fan amid the landscape of the lakes and the mountains. It is Zhujiajiao. Zhujiajiao is located at the junction of Jiangsu, Zhejiang, and Shanghai, with the Caogang River flowing through the town amid its well-connected waterways. It is Shanghai's gateway to the Beijing-Hangzhou Grand Canal. The area was already inhabited 5,000 years ago, forming a market town during the Song and Yuan dynasties, and becoming a major trading town in the Yangtze River Delta during the Ming and Qing dynasties when it gathered grain-transporting ships and thousands of households. During the Republic of China, modern commerce and industry flourished, when the city was known as the "Venice of Shanghai". It is also the birthplace of the Boat Boxing in the south of the Yangtze River, which was once feared by pirates, especially those from Japan in the 16th and 17th centuries. Almost every family here practiced the boxing techniques one hundred years ago, which has been passed generation after generation. The boat boxing, which incorporates the Wu state army's water warfare techniques, the Shaolin Temple's Plum Blossom Stake, and others, has formed its own school of martial arts. With this boxing, one can move around within the narrow bow of a ship and win over the enemies. As a result, it is a great skill for the people transporting the grain to safeguard their ships and families. During the street tours on the Dragon Boat Festival every year, the boat boxing performances under the Fangsheng (Releasing Living Creatures) Bridge win huge applauses. Constructed in the Ming Dynasty, the Fangsheng Bridge has been known as the "first bridge in Shanghai". It is the largest five-hole stone bridge in the south of the Yangtze River. Standing at the top of the bridge to watch the fast-rowed boat race, you will see hundreds of boats competing in the river, with paddles flying and golden drums beaten amid a riot of excitement.

第二章
Chapter 2

徽派民居
Huizhou-Style Residential Buildings

安徽
Anhui

宏村：浓淡相宜，画里乡村
Hongcun Village: Picturesque Village Appealing with Either Light or Heavy Make-up

  黟县宏村始建于南宋，现存明清古建百余座，科学美观的人工水系堪称一绝，是徽派建筑的典范。古村背倚黄山余脉，地势较高，常若云蒸霞蔚，村中清溪绕舍，白墙灰瓦掩映于远山近水之中，浓淡相宜，人文与自然景观高度融合，正所谓"青山不墨千年画，流水无弦万里琴"，是真正的"中国画里的乡村"。

  村首南湖是宏村先人仿西湖平湖秋月式样而建，青莲碧水，湖心那玉带一般的画桥，李慕白曾牵马走过。跨过画桥，便是南湖书院，琅琅书声传承着千年文明。走入村中，处处是高高的飞檐，错落的马头墙，古朴庄重。步入宅院，别致的天井、花园、漏窗、房梁，典雅的对额、石墩、盆景、家具，无言诠释着徽派建筑家的匠心。乐叙堂的"五凤楼"、承志堂的绣楼、树人堂的木雕，富丽恢宏，巧夺天工，展示了徽州"三雕"艺术之绝美。古村中心是最美的月沼，一弯半月状的碧水中天光云影徘徊。塘呈半月蕴含着先人的智慧：月满则亏，凡事皆需留有余地。

  Located in Yixian County of Anhui Province, Hongcun Village was built in the Southern Song Dynasty. It has preserved more than one hundred ancient buildings of the Ming and Qing dynasties. With its exceptional scientific and beautiful artificial water system, it is a model of Huizhou-style architecture. Backed by the stretching branch of Mount Huangshan, the ancient village has a high terrain that often sees rosy clouds slowly rising. In the village, clear streams surround the houses, whose white walls and grey tiles are looming against the distant mountains and water. Being appealing with either light or heavy makeup, it sees its humanistic and natural landscape highly integrated. As a saying goes, "the green hills, without ink, are paintings lasting for millennia. The flowing water, without strings, are like zithers with sounds spreading thousands of miles." It is a true "countryside in the traditional Chinese painting".

  At the entrance of the village is the Nanhu (South) Lake, which was built by the ancestors of Hongcun Village in imitation of the scenic spot of "an autumn moon over the calm lake" in the West Lake. Surrounded by green lotus leaves and azure water, the Huaqiao (Painted) Bridge, which looks like a jade belt on the heart of the lake, was stepped by Li Mubai (the protagonist in An Lee's movie *Crouching Tiger, Hidden Dragon*)

leading a horse. On the other side of the Painted Bridge is the Nanhu Lake (South Lake) Academy, where the ringing sounds of reading aloud have been passing down the civilization which has lasted for millennia. After sauntering into the village, you will see overhanging eaves and staggered corbiesteps everywhere amid a simple and dignified ambiance. As you enter the house, you are greeted by the unconventional patio, gardens, leaking windows, beams, elegant couplets, stone piers, potted landscape, and furniture. All of them are silent manifestations of the craftsmanship of the Huizhou architects. The "Wufeng (Five Phoenix) Buildings" in the Lexu (Joyous Chatting) Hall, the Xiulou (Embroidered) Building in the Chengzhi (Ambition-Inheriting) Hall and the wooden carvings in the Shuren (People-Nurturing) Hall are beautiful and magnificent, which reveal the superb craftsmanship excelling nature and demonstrate the beauty of the "triple carvings" of Huizhou. In the center of the ancient village is the most beautiful crescent marsh. The crescent-shaped blue water reflects the sky and clouds above. The crescent-shaped pond contains the wisdom of the ancestors: As the moon waxes only to wane, we should allow for the unpredictable in every matter.

西递：诗礼桃源，民居典范
Xidi: Poetic and Ritualistic Land of Peace and Happiness and Model of Folk Residential Buildings

自宏村南行约二十千米，便可至西递。西递四面环山、双溪穿村，素有"桃花源里人家"之美誉。西递始建于北宋，是明经胡氏聚居地，清初臻于鼎盛，目前西递基本保留了明清时期的风貌格局，有百余幢明清古建存留完好，被誉为"中国明清民居博物馆"。村首矗立着明代胡文光刺史牌楼，高十三米，全用本地"黟县青"制成，雕琢精绝，巍峨峥嵘，为我国石坊建筑之瑰宝。漫步村中，层楼叠院、巷贯街连，大宅富丽恢宏，小院精巧舒适，其"布局之工，结构之巧，装饰之美，营造之精，文化内涵之深"，堪称徽派建筑典范。胡氏先人还创造性地将家族文化融入建筑之中，通过精湛多姿的三雕，发人深省的楹联、格言、题额和漏窗来传承家训。悬于瑞玉庭的"快乐每从辛苦得，便宜多自吃亏来"是一副错字联："辛"字多了一横，寓意多付出一份辛苦，就能多收获一份体现自我价值的快乐；"亏"字多了一点，多吃一些亏，往往便能获得更大的便宜。楹联生动地传递了徽商的处世哲学，润物无声地熏陶着后人。

After traveling for about 20 kilometers southward from Hongcun Village, you will reach Xidi. Surrounded by mountains and with two streams flowing through, Xidi has been known as a "living land of peace and happiness". Xidi was built in the Northern Song Dynasty as a settlement of the Hu Clan who were adept at Confucian classics. It reached its peak in the early Qing Dynasty. At present, Xidi has basically retained its pattern of the Ming and Qing Dynasty. With more than a hundred well-preserved ancient buildings of the Ming and Qing dynasties, it has been known as the "museum of Ming and Qing folk residences in China". At the head of the village stands the Decorated Archway of Provincial Governor Hu Wenguang in the Ming Dynasty. With a height of thirteen meters, it was made entirely with the local "green bricks of Yixian County". Exquisitely carved and lofty, it is a treasure of Chinese stone arch buildings. Sauntering through the village, you will see the overlapping buildings and courtyards and connected streets and alleys. The large mansions are magnificent, while the small courtyards are exquisite and comfortable. They can be hailed as models of Huizhou architecture for their "skillful workmanship, exquisite structures, beautiful decoration, refined construction, and profound cultural connotations." The ancestors of the Hu Clan also creatively integrated their family culture into the buildings, passing on family precepts through exquisite and colorful triple carvings, and thought-provoking couplets, mottos, inscriptions, and leaking windows. The couplets hanging in the Ruiyu (Auspicious Jade) Courtyard read, "Happiness comes from hard work, and conveniences come from suffering losses." The couplets contain some wrong words: the word "hard" has an extra "h," implying that by putting in more hard work, one can reap more happiness that reflects one's own value; the word "loss" has an extra "l" which means that if you suffer more losses, you can often get a greater advantage. The couplets vividly convey the philosophy of the Huizhou merchants in conducting themselves, which silently inculcates future generations.

03 卢村：木雕楼群，徽派精华
Lucun Village: Buildings with Wooden Carvings, Reflecting the Essence of the Huizhou Style

　　三四月间，自宏村北行三里，在一大片娇美无匹的鹅黄花田之畔，一幢幢错落有致的水墨民居临水而立，屋设敞廊、廊边美人靠，溪上五步一桥、十步一亭，恍若苏杭水乡，这便是卢村了。自南唐末年卢氏先祖迁居到这块"双溪相抱，青山为靠"的宝地，延续至今已有千年。卢村现存明清民居四十九幢，其中最闻名遐迩的是卢氏三十三世祖卢邦燮建于清道光年间的木雕楼群，它集徽派建筑精华之大成，被誉为"中国木雕第一楼"。木雕楼群由七家里民居组成，包括志诚堂、思济堂、玻璃厅等宅院。光志诚堂就花了两位巧匠20年的工夫，采用浅雕、深雕、镂空雕等多种技法，方寸之间人物意态尽显、花鸟纤毫毕现，尤其特别是表现主人生平功业的战事图，精心描绘了鸦片战争和太平天国运动的历史场景，生动逼真，极具价值。

In March and April, after traveling for three li northward from Hongcun Village, you will come to a large field of exceptionally beautiful light yellow flowers. Residential buildings stand waterside around you in attractive disorder as if coming from ink paintings. On their open corridors, you will sometimes spot beautiful women leaning. Along the streams, you will see a bridge and a pavilion here and there, as if being in a waterside town in Suzhou and Hangzhou. You are in Lucun Village. Over one thousand years have passed since the end of the Southern Tang Dynasty of the Five Dynasties (907-960) and Ten Kingdoms (902-979) when the ancestors of the Lu Clan relocated to this precious place "embraced by two streams and backed by green mountains". Forty-nine residential buildings have been preserved in Lucun Village, the most famous ones of which are the Buildings of Wooden Carving built by Lu Bangxie, the 33rd ancestor of the Lu Clan, during Emperor Daoguang's reign (1821–1850) in the Qing Dynasty. As an epitome of the essentials of Huizhou-style architecture, they have been hailed as "the first buildings of wooden carving in China". The Buildings of Wooden Carvings consist of seven residential buildings, including the Zhicheng (Ambition and Sincerity) Hall, the Siji (Relieving-Yearning) Hall, the Glass Hall, and other buildings and courtyards. It took two master craftsmen 20 years of work to carve the Ambition and Sincerity Hall alone. Using a variety of techniques such as low relief, deep engraving, and openwork carving, they reveal the bearings of the figures and the details of flowers and birds within a confined space. In particular, such efforts are emphasized in the battle scenes showing glorious deeds of the owners, carefully depicting the historical scenes of the Opium War (1840–1842) and the Taiping Movement (1843–1864). Being vivid and realistic, they are highly valuable.

04 南屏：巍巍祠堂，幽幽曲巷
Nanping: Lofty Ancestral Halls and Tranquil Winding Lanes

在皖南黟县西南处，有一座山环水绕的千年古村，曲径通幽、风景如画，因背倚南屏山而得今名"南屏"。南屏原名叶村，明代已形成叶、程、李三大宗族齐聚分治的格局，清中叶以后随着徽商的崛起步入鼎盛，官商学三位一体，人杰辈出。各宗族皆建祠堂，逐渐形成了规模壮观的祠堂群。村中至今仍保留着八座祠堂，有宏大的宗祠、支祠，也有小巧的家祠，被誉为"中国古祠堂建筑博物馆"。始建于明代的叶氏宗祠叙秩堂位于古村中心，开阔轩敞、气势恢宏，张艺谋的电影《菊豆》就取景于此。村中三百余幢明清民居错落有致，七十二道高墙深巷回环往复，游客到此，仿佛穿越时空，堕入一个古典秀美的迷宫。

In the southwest of Yixian County in southern Anhui, there is a millennium-old village surrounded by mountains and rivers and featuring winding paths leading to tranquil and picturesque scenery. Backed by the Nanping (Southern Screen) Mountain, it is called "Nanping" at present. Nanping was originally named Yecun Village. In the Ming Dynasty, three clans, including Ye, Cheng, and Li, had already formed the pattern of gathering and managing the village together. After the middle of the Qing Dynasty, with the rise of the Huizhou merchants, the village ushered in its prosperity. With the trio of officials, merchants, and scholars, it has witnessed talents emerging in large numbers. Ancestral halls were built by each clan, gradually giving rise to a spectacular cluster of ancestral halls. There are still eight ancestral halls in the village, ranging from grand clan ancestral halls and branch ones to small family ones. With these, it has been known as the "museum of Chinese ancient ancestral hall buildings". Built in the Ming Dynasty, the Ancestral Hall of the Ye Clan, known as the Xuzhi Hall, is located in the center of the ancient village. It is spacious and magnificent, being the setting for the film *Ju Dou* directed by Zhang Yimou (a Chinese movie director). In the village are over three hundred residential buildings of the Ming and Qing dynasties in attractive disorder. Seventy-two high walls and deep alleys are in zigzags and loops. Here, visitors are transported through time and space into a maze of classical beauty.

屏山：青山画屏，古桥落虹
Pingshan: Green Hills Looking Like Painted Screens and Ancient Bridges Resembling Fallen Rainbows

在世界文化遗产西递和宏村之间，有一座秀美如诗、静默如画的千年古村，因村北高山状如画屏而得名屏山。古村山环水绕，吉阳溪贯村而过，白墙青瓦夹岸林立，古朴石桥跨溪如虹；长宁湖波光粼粼，天光水色相映成趣，松柏桃柳四时皆景。屏山村明清建制时曾属徽州府黟县九都，且是舒姓聚居地，故又称九都舒村。舒姓相传是伏羲氏九世孙叔子的后裔，自唐末迁居到此已有一千一百多年了。舒氏诗礼传家，自古人才辈出，至今存留祠堂七座，明清民居二百余幢，其中红庙、舒绣文故居、玉兰厅等都是经典的徽派建筑。

Between the world intangible cultural heritage sites of Xidi Village and Hongcun Village, there is a millennium-old ancient village as beautiful as poetry and as tranquil as painting. It is named Pingshan (Screen Mountain) because a high mountain in the north of the village resembles a painted screen. The ancient village is surrounded by mountains and rivers. The Jiyang (Auspicious Sun) Stream flows through the village, with white walls and green tiles lining the banks. Ancient stone bridges, which look like rainbows, span the river. The Changning (Lasting Tranquility) Lake is sparkling, where the sky and water reflect each other. Trees, including the pines, cypresses, peaches, and willows, present scenic sights all year round. Pingshan Village was a part of Jiudu, Yixian County, Huizhou Prefecture when it was established in the Ming and Qing dynasties. It was also known as Jiudushu Village because it was an inhabited land for the people surnamed Shu. The people surnamed Shu are said to be descendants of Shuzi, the ninth grandson of the Fuxi (legendary Chinese emperor from 2852 to 2738 BC) Clan. They have been living here for more than 1,100 years since they relocated here at the end of the Tang Dynasty. The lineage of the Shu Clan has been sustained through culture for generations. There have been preserved seven ancestral halls and over 200 residential buildings from the Ming and Qing dynasties, including the Hongmiao (Red) Temple, the Former Residence of Shu Xiuwen, the Yulan (Magnolia) Hall, and other classic Huizhou-style buildings.

关麓：亦儒亦商，翰墨书香
Guanlu: Land of Scholars and Merchants amid Cultural Fragrance

关麓村静卧于皖南黟城盆地的青山绿野间，因地处"西武雄关"西武岭东麓而得名。唐朝名臣汪华的后裔于此聚族而居，历经千年沧桑之变，关麓至今仍是一幅"暧暧远人村，依依墟里烟"的田园景色。清代时随着徽商的崛起，关麓逐渐走向繁盛，屋宇连绵气势不凡。至今留存的古民居中，最具特色的是汪氏八兄弟的连体古建"八大家"。它始建于清顺治年间，历经二百余年方建成，以清代书画名家汪曙故居武亭山居领首，是徽派联幢民居的传世杰作。八家宅第自成一体又相互联通，浑然一体又各有千秋，其结构之精妙，建筑之华美，令人叹服。汪氏世代书香，村中书屋学厅极多，步入村中仿佛走进了古代私塾文化博物馆，充分体现了徽商"亦儒亦商"的传统。

Guanlu Village lies quietly among the green hills and fields of the Yicheng basin in southern Anhui. It is named after its location at the eastern foot of Xiwu Ridge which is also known as the "Strong Pass of Xiwu". The descendants of Wang Hua (586–649), a famous minister of the Tang Dynasty, lived here as a clan. After one thousand years of vicissitudes, Guanlu still features idyllic scenes that "In the distance loom villages under the dim skylight. Lingering is the cooking smoke from the settlements". With the rise of the Huizhou Merchants in the Qing Dynasty, Guanlu gradually became prosperous, with undulating buildings revealing a majestic outlook. The most distinctive of the ancient residential buildings that have survived to date is the "Eight-Great-Family Complex," the terraced ancient complex of the eight brothers of the Wang's Family. It was built during Emperor Shunzhi's reign (1644–1662) of the Qing Dynasty and took more than 200 years to complete. Led by the Wuting Mountain Building, which is the Former Residence of Wang Shu, a famous calligrapher and painter of the Qing Dynasty, the complex is an heirloom masterpiece of the Huizhou school of terraced residential buildings. The eight manors are self-contained and interconnected, being integrated and distinctive. You will gasp in admiration for their structural exquisiteness and architectural splendor. The lineage of the Wang Clan has been passed on through culture. There are many study halls in the village. Strolling into the village, you will feel like walking into a museum of the ancient private school culture. It has fully reflected the scholarly tradition of the Huizhou merchants.

07 呈坎：负阴抱阳，国宝之乡
Chengkan: Home of National Treasures amid Well-Balanced Yin and Yang

呈坎地处黄山南麓青山绿水间，是罗姓聚居地。三国时东吴人到此见八面环山，长河穿村、百溪汇聚，犹如"九龙戏珠"，便定居于此，易名龙溪，并按照易理来布局建村，融人文八卦于山水八卦之中。唐末罗氏先祖迁居此地，据"阳呈阴坎"的易经思想将村名改为"呈坎"。罗氏家族人文荟萃，宋代理学家朱熹曾赞道"呈坎双贤里，江南第一村"。明清时期随着徽商的发展和程朱理学的浸润，又经治理营建，呈坎的建筑更加精致严整，风水格局更趋完美。如今呈坎布局未改，存留历代古建150余处，其中明代民居30余幢，仅举世罕见的明代三层楼就有7幢，是我国保存最完整的明代古村落。呈坎古建类型丰富、风格独特，三雕精绝、彩绘鲜妍，被誉为"中国古建筑艺术博物馆"。

Located among the green hills and clear rivers at the southern foot of Mount Huangshan, Chengkan is an inhabited land for those surnamed Luo. During the Three Kingdoms period (220–280), the people of the Eastern Wu State came here where they saw that it was surrounded by mountains on all sides, with a long river flowing through and numerous streams converging. The sight is like that "nine dragons playing with a pearl". As a result, they settled down here, changed its name to Longxi (Dragon Stream), and built the village according to the principle of the *Book of Changes*, integrating the humanistic eight trigrams into the natural eight trigrams. At the end of the Tang Dynasty, the ancestors of those surnamed Luo moved here. They changed the name of the village to "Chengkan" based on the idea of "Cheng for Yang" and "Kan for Yin" in the *Book of Changes*. The Luo Clan features a rich cultural heritage. "Chengkan is the hometown of two exceptionally virtuous figures and the first village of the south of the Yangtze River," praised Zhu Xi (1130–1200, founder of Neo-Confucianism) in the Song Dynasty. During the Ming and Qing dynasties, with the development of the Huizhou merchants, the infusion of Neo-Confucianism, and the construction and governance, the buildings of Chengkan is more exquisite and orderly, with a more perfect geomancy pattern. At present, Chengkan has maintained its layout, having preserved more than 150 ancient buildings of the past eras, including over 30 residential buildings of the Ming Dynasty. There are seven rare three-story buildings of the Ming Dynasty. It is the ancient village with the most complete preservation of buildings of the Ming Dynasty throughout China. Chengkan's ancient buildings feature various types, unique styles, exquisite triple carvings, and bright-colored paintings, enabling it to be hailed as a "museum of Chinese ancient architectural art".

08 唐模：水口园林，风姿天然
Tangmo: Estuary-side Garden with Natural Graceful Bearing

　　距呈坎十里之遥，是徽州又一座风姿天然的千年古村唐模。其始建者为唐朝越国公汪华的曾祖父。徽派村落特重水口，而唐模最独特之处就是将水口与园林完美融合，形成水口园林的杰作——檀干园。檀干溪穿过檀干园流贯全村，夹岸粉墙黛瓦错落有致。胸有丘壑的造园人充分利用了天然的湖山坡地，堆土为山、挑堤种柳，园中"门楼知稼，廊庑连芸"，将山水、田园、村舍融为一体，形成一个"全村同在画中居"的桃花源。檀干园是清代孝子许以诚为遂母亲心愿仿西湖景致而建，故又称小西湖、孝子湖。唐模不仅出孝子，更出才子。久负盛名的同胞牌坊便是康熙皇帝为表彰同中进士的许家双生兄弟而恩准建造的。这座牌坊是三间三楼四柱式，规格很高，气势恢宏。石雕精绝传神、寓意深刻，是古牌坊中的经典之作。

　　Ten li away from Chengkan is Tangmo, another millennium-old village with a natural graceful bearing in Huizhou. It was first built by the great-grandfather of Wang Hua (586–649), the Duke of Yue state in the Tang Dynasty. Huizhou-style villages place a special emphasis on estuaries. The most unique feature of Tangmo is the perfect fusion of the estuary and the garden, forming the Tan'gan Garden, a masterpiece of estuary gardens. The Tan'gan River flows past the Tan'gan Garden and through the village, with its banks lined with white walls and grey tiles in attractive disorder. Garden makers, who are circumspect and far-sighted, made full use of the natural slopes of the lake and mountains. They piled up earth to make hills and planted willows on the embankments. In the garden, "the gatehouses see crops, while the corridors are connected like clouds," blending the landscape, the fields, and the village house into one, forming a land of peace and prosperity where "the whole village lives as if in a painting." The Tan'gan Garden was built by Xu Yicheng, a filial son in the Qing Dynasty, in response to his mother's wish to imitate the scenery of the West Lake. It has therefore been also known as the Little West Lake and the Lake of a Filial Son. Tangmo not only produces filial children, but also talented persons. The long reputable Sibling Memorial Arch was built by a decree of Emperor Kangxi in honor of the twin brothers of the Xu's Family, who were both successful candidates of the imperial civil examination at the highest level. This memorial arch is a three-bay, three-story, and four-pillar structure of exceptional specification and grandeur. With superbly evocative stone carvings and profound connotations, it is a classic work among ancient memorial arches.

09 棠樾：慈孝无双，牌坊之乡
Tangyue: The Hometown of Memorial Arches with Unparalleled Love and Filial Piety

"一生痴绝处，无梦到徽州"。牌坊、祠堂、民居，并称徽州三绝。牌坊作为封建社会最高荣誉的象征，是徽派文化辉煌的缩影。歙县棠樾古村便是以七重明清牌坊名扬天下。站在棠樾村口，便可看到七座高大华美牌坊依序排列在曲折有致的石板路上，逶迤成群，视角不同构图千变万化，春天巍峨耸立于无涯的金黄花田间，那种美一见难忘。这七座明清牌坊勾勒出了儒家"忠、孝、节、义"的伦理概貌，也见证了徽商官商一体纵横三百年的雄厚实力。每一座牌坊背后都有一个感人肺腑的传奇，乾隆皇帝曾褒奖牌坊的主人鲍氏家族，称其为"慈孝天下无双里，衮绣江南第一乡"。走过七重牌坊，眼前是三座恢宏典雅的祠堂，其中清懿堂是专为棠樾女性而设的女祠，这在封建社会举世无双，堪称石破天惊的奇迹。

"My lifetime is infatuated with exceptional destinations, but I have not yet dreamt about such a fine place like Huizhou." The memorial arches, ancestral halls, and residential buildings are known as the three exceptional items in Huizhou. As symbols of the highest honor in feudal society, memorial arches are the epitome of the splendor of Huizhou culture. The ancient village of Tangyue in Shexian County is famous for its seven memorial arches of the Ming and Qing dynasties. Standing at the entrance of Tangyue Village, you can see seven towering and gorgeous memorial arches arranged in order on the winding stone road. They wind to form a group, showing different compositions from different perspectives. In spring, they tower over the vast stretches of golden flowers, revealing a truly unforgettable beautiful sight. The seven memorial arches of the Ming and Qing dynasties outline the Confucian ethics of "loyalty, filial piety, integrity, and righteousness" and bear witness to the strength of the Huizhou merchants who are also officials and scholars to flourish in a course of three hundred years. Behind every memorial arch is a soul-stirring legend. Emperor Qianlong once praised the Bao family, the owners of the memorial arch, as "the town with unparalleled love and filial piety across the country, the first town with formally dressed officials in the south of the Yangtze River." Walking past the seven memorial arches, you will see three magnificent and elegant ancestral halls, including the Qingyi (Clear Virtue) Hall, a women's ancestral hall dedicated to the women of Tangyue. Unparalleled in feudal society, it is considered an extraordinarily surprising miracle.

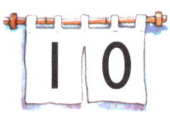

10 查济：桃花流水，别有天地
Zhaji: A Different Land with Peach Blossoms and Flowing Water

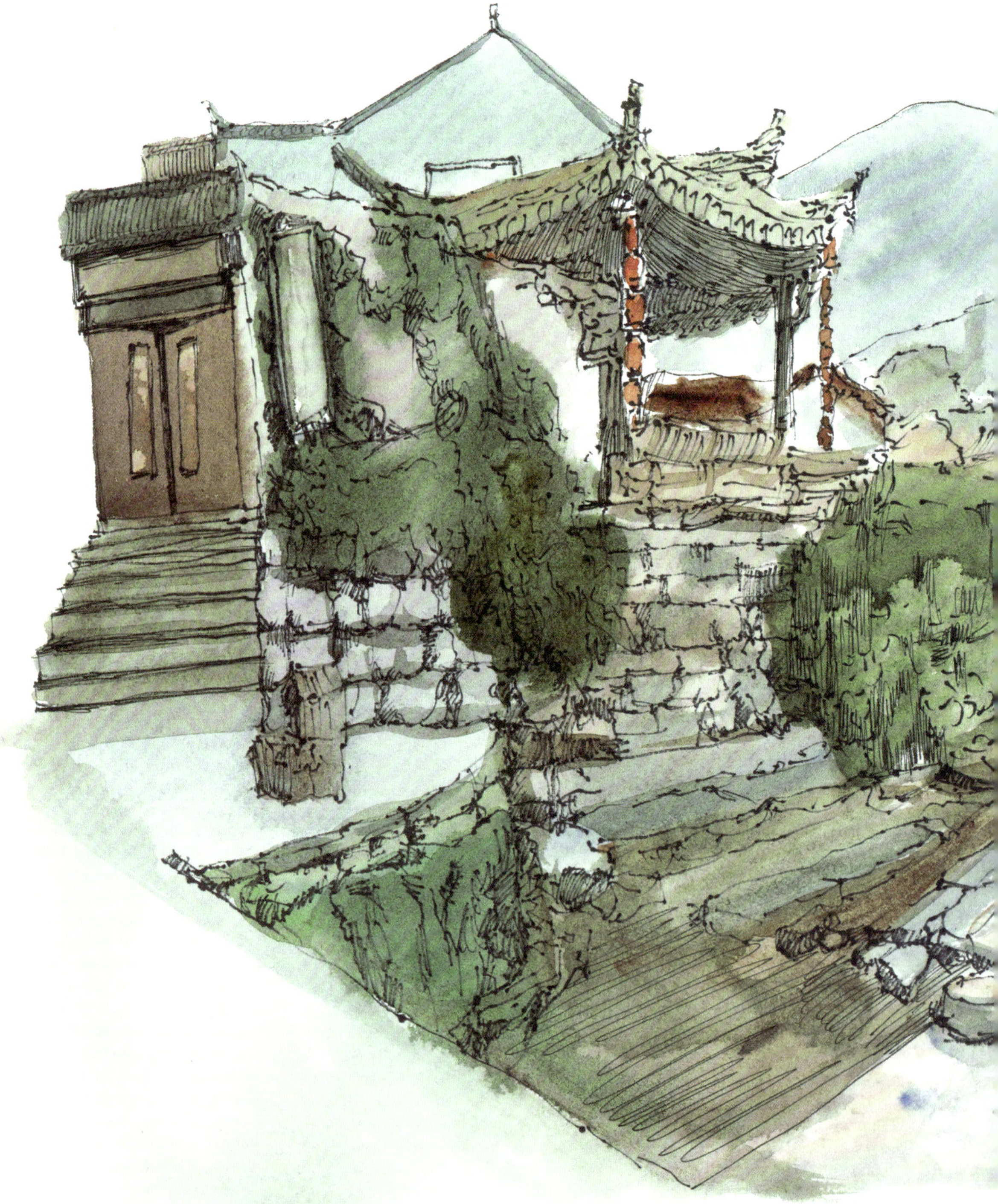

离桃花潭四十余里，是皖南最大的明清古村落查济，这里是武侠大家金庸（查良镛）的故乡，由查氏先祖文熙公于唐朝初年始建。古村四面环山、三溪汇流，四门三塔相映成趣，风景独一无二。诗仙李白在游历查济的石门碧山之后，留下了"问余何意栖碧山，笑而不答心自闲。桃花流水窅然去，别有天地非人间"的千古名篇。明朝中叶，查济臻于鼎盛，人烟十万，宅第如云。查济原有桥梁、祠堂、庙宇各一百零八座，如今尚存古建一百四十余处。德公厅屋是唯一残存的元代建筑，屋内十六根珍贵的楠木柱见证了昔日辉煌。村中断壁残垣极多，所幸民居格局未变，依旧是一幅"门外青山如屋里，东家流水入西邻"的和谐画面。

More than 40 li from Taohua (Peach Blossom) Pool is Zhaji, the largest ancient village of the Ming and Qing dynasties in southern Anhui. It is the hometown of the renowned martial arts novelist Jin Yong (1924–2018, also known as Zha Liangyong). It was first built by Duke Wenxi, the ancestor of the Zha Clan, in the early Tang Dynasty. The ancient village is surrounded by mountains. With three streams converging, and four gates and three pagodas complementing each other, this village features a unique landscape. The poet-immortal Li Bai (701–762), after visiting Bishan, Shimen in Zhaji, left behind a reputable poem for millennia, which reads, "I dwell among green hills and someone asks me why, my mind carefree, I smile and give him no reply. Peach blossoms fallen on running water pass by, this is an earthly paradise beneath the sky." In the middle of the Ming Dynasty, Zhaji was at its pinnacle, with a population of over 100,000 living in manors as many as clouds. There were 108 bridges, 108 ancestral halls, and 108 temples in Zhaji, and over 140 ancient buildings remaining today. As the only remaining building from the Yuan Dynasty, the Degong (Virtuous Lord) Hall has sixteen precious Phoebe nanmu pillars as testaments to its former glory. There are many broken walls in the village, but fortunately, the pattern of the residential buildings remains unchanged, still maintaining a harmonious picture in which "green hills outside the door look like something indoor; water flows from the eastern neighborhoods into the western ones."

三河：江淮水乡，土菜飘香
Sanhe: Waterside Town with the Fragrance of Local Cuisines in the Yangtze-Huaihe River Valley

　　三河古镇旧称鹊渚，数千年前原是古巢湖中的一个小洲，渐因泥沙淤积成陆。三河地处肥西、庐江、舒城三县交界处，丰乐河、杭埠河、小南河三水流贯其间，自古便是水陆通衢，明清时期百货交通、商贾云集，是皖中商贸首镇，清末民初商业更是盛极一时，有"小上海"之称，李鸿章家族的钱庄、粮仓就建在三河。走在古街上，看那一座座前铺后宅的徽式合院、一块块黑漆鎏金的店招匾额，仍可想见昔日的无限繁华。因水陆皆是咽喉要道，三河自古便是兵家必争之地。军事史上著名的鹊岸之战、鹊尾之战、三河大捷，都在这座千年古镇留下了烽火遗迹。而今古镇最吸引八方来客的还有它的美食文化，三河土菜以徽派菜系为底蕴，据地域之便、融南北之长，令人回味无穷。土菜价格极为公道，体现着三河人"仁爱为本，诚信立世"的传统徽商精神。

　　The ancient town of Sanhe, formerly known as Quezhu (Magpie Islet), was originally a small islet in the ancient Chaohu Lake millennia ago, but it gradually silted up into land due to sedimentation. Sanhe is located at the junction of Feixi, Lujiang, Shucheng counties. With Fengle River, Hangbu River, and Xiaonan River flowing through, it has been a land and water thoroughfare since ancient times. In the Ming and Qing dynasties, with the gathering of various goods and merchants, it was the first commercial town in Anhui. In the late Qing Dynasty and early Republic of China, it was greatly prosperous, earning itself the title of "small Shanghai". The money house and granary of the clan of Li Hongzhang (1823–1901, an ancient Chinese general, politician, and diplomat) were built in Sanhe. Walking along the old street, you will see the Huizhou-style courtyards with front shops and rear residential buildings. From the black-lacquered and gilt shop signs, you can still imagine their unlimited past prosperity. With its water and land routes being strategic passages, Sanhe has been a hotly contested place. Famous battles in military history, such as the Battle of Quean, the Battle of Quewei, and the Great Victory of Sanhe, have left their beacon relics in this millennium-old town. At present, the ancient town's most attractive feature for visitors from all directions is its culinary culture. With the Huizhou cuisine as its foundation, the local cuisine of Sanhe also takes advantage of its convenient geographical location and absorbs the merits of cuisines of the south and the north, producing lingering tastes. The prices of the local cuisine are extremely fair, reflecting the traditional Huizhou merchants' spirit of the people of Sanhe to "take benevolence and love as the foundation and to conduct themselves with credibility."

江西
Jiangxi

瑶里：瓷源茶乡，林海雪瀑
Yaoli: Cradle of Porcelain and a Hometown of Tea amid Forest Seas and Snow Waterfalls

瑶里古镇位于世界瓷都景德镇东南端，古镇南踞象山、北卧狮山，一条澄澈的瑶河贯穿东西，两岸的徽派水墨民居倒影如画，青山绿水间流淌着明清古韵。古巷中隐藏着中西合璧的徽派合院"狮冈胜览"和三雕精绝的程氏宗祠。瑶里始建于西汉，旧称"窑里"，因是景德瓷器的发祥地而得名，远在唐代中叶就因瓷窑闻名，宋元明时制瓷业达到顶峰。"高岭土，窑里釉"，瑶里高岭山独有的高岭土是烧景德瓷的关键原料。走在古镇绕南一带，时见古老的瓷窑遗址，可遥想当年"十万陶工，万炮齐轰"的盛况。古镇茶坊如星散落，春来到此品一杯崖玉新茶，神清气爽。瑶里不仅是"瓷之源、茶之乡"，还是"林之海"。古镇依傍梅岭和汪湖，既有飞瀑流泉、奇石洞天，又有千年樟群、原始密林，宛如绿色仙境。

Located at the south-eastern end of Jingdezhen, the world's porcelain capital, Yaoli Ancient Town is perched on Xiangshan (Elephant) Mountain in the south and Shishan (Lion) Mountain in the north, with the clear Yaoli River flowing through its east and west, reflecting picturesque houses as if coming from an ink painting on both banks. Between the green hills and the azure water, it flows with the antique appeal of the Ming and Qing dynasties. Among its ancient lanes are Shigang Shenglan (A Hearty View of the Lion Mountain) as a Huizhou-style courtyard blending Chinese and Western styles, and the Ancestral Hall of the Cheng Clan featuring the exceptionally exquisite triple carvings. Founded in the Western Han Dynasty (202 BC–220 AD), Yaoli was formerly known as "Yaoli" (inside the kiln) named after its being the birthplace of porcelain in Jingdezhen. It became famous for its porcelain kilns as far back as the mid-Tang Dynasty, with its porcelain production reaching its pinnacle during the Song, Yuan, and Ming dynasties. There is a saying about "the kaolin clay and the Yaoli glaze". The unique kaolin clay from the Gaoling Mountains in Yaoli is a key raw material for firing porcelain in Jingdezhen. While touring around the Raonan area of the town, you will see the ruins of ancient porcelain kilns and think back to the days when "100,000 potters fired 10,000 burning stoves". Tea houses in the ancient town are scattered like stars. In spring, you can come here to taste a cup of Yayu new tea and refresh yourself. Yaoli is not only the "cradle of porcelain and the hometown of tea," but also the "sea of forests". The ancient town is located near Meiling (Plum) Ridge and Wanghu (Vast) Lake, with waterfalls, springs, grotesque rocks, and caves. It also has millennium-old camphor trees amid its pristine forests, making it a green wonderland.

富田：碧血丹心，红星闪耀
Futian: Patriotic Heart like a Shining Red Star

"人生自古谁无死，留取丹心照汗青。"文天祥的铿锵之语激励着古往今来无数仁人志士。他的故乡，便是位于江西吉安的富田古镇。富田是庐陵文化的重要发祥地，始建于三国，距今已有一千八百年的历史，宋元明清历代建筑皆有留存。走进文丞相祠堂和陵园，一股"下则为河岳，上则为日星"的浩然正气涤荡着灵魂。建于明代的诚敬堂是富田另一座名祠，祠中繁复典丽的木质建筑皆以木榫衔接，结构精妙、气势宏阔，有"江南第一祠"的美誉。富田曾是中央苏区革命活动的中心，毛泽东、朱德、陈毅等老一辈革命家在这里留下了众多战斗和生活遗址。红星闪耀，革命精神永远激励着后人。

"Since olden days there's never been a man but dies; I'd leave a loyalist's name in history only." The resounding words of Wen Tianxiang (1236–1283, an ancient Chinese politician and poet) have inspired countless people with lofty ideals throughout the ages. His hometown is the ancient town of Futian in Ji'an, Jiangxi Province. As an important birthplace of Luling culture, Futian was built in the Three Kingdoms period (220–280), with a history of 1,800 years. It has buildings that survived from the Song, Yuan, Ming, and Qing dynasties. When you walk into the ancestral hall and mausoleum of Prime Minister Wen, the lofty spirit of "being the rivers and the mountains below, and the sun and the stars above" cleanses souls. Built in the Ming Dynasty, the Chengjing (Sincerity and Respect) Hall is another famous ancestral hall in Futian. The intricate wooden buildings have wooden mortise and tenon joints. Featuring a delicate structure and a magnificent style, it has been hailed as the "first ancestral hall in the south of the Yangtze River." Futian was once a center of revolutionary activities in the Central Chinese Soviet Area, where veteran revolutionaries such as Mao Zedong (1893–1976, Chinese Communist leader and founder of the PRC), Zhu De (1886–1976, Chinese Communist leader and founder of the People's Liberation Army), and Chen Yi (1901–1972, Chinese Communist general and politician) left numerous battling and living traces. The Red Star shines brightly, with the revolutionary spirit always inspiring future generations.

流坑：科甲联芳，千古一村
Liukeng: Famous Village for All Eternity with Multiple Successful Candidates of the Imperial Civil Examinations at the Highest Level

江西乐安流坑村，坐落于乌江之畔、青山环抱的盆地之中。古村沿乌江设立"七竖一横"的街巷，七条竖巷皆建望楼和码头，既享舟楫之利，又便于防御。这种"活水排形"的结构，还能使整个村庄江风相拂、清流贯通，深具"天人合一"的风水之妙。流坑为董氏单姓聚居地，自南唐五代一世祖董合迁居于此，弹指间千载已过。董氏家族诗书继世，在科举史上曾出过文武状元各一名，进士三十四名，举人七十八名，创造了耕读文明的辉煌奇迹。两宋尤为人才井喷期，曾有一科同中五名进士。如今纪念"五子登科"的五桂坊已渺然无踪，但始建于南宋的状元楼仍巍巍屹立，见证着董氏当年科甲联芳、仕宦如云的盛景。明清流坑人以竹木贸易富甲一方，留下无数绝美的建筑和文物。流坑山水形胜，其科举之盛、仕宦之众、经商之富、家族之大、延续之久，无愧于"千古第一村"的美誉。

Located in Le'an, Jiangxi Province, Liukeng Village is in a basin on the banks of the Wujiang River and is surrounded by green mountains. The village has seven vertical streets and one horizontal street along the Wujiang River, with the seven vertical streets built with watchtowers and piers, providing the benefits of water transport and the conveniences for defense. In addition, the structure of "arranging the layout according to the flowing water" allows the whole village to be caressed by the river breeze and to be connected by the clear stream. It has deeply reflected the wonderful geomancy featuring the "Unity of Heaven and humanity." Liukang is an inhabited land only with the people surnamed Dong. Over one thousand years have passed since Dong He (around the tenth century), the first ancestor during the Tang of the Five Southern Dynasties relocated here. The Dong Clan has been passed on through culture. In the history of the imperial civil examinations, the Dong Clan produced one top cultural and one top military candidate of the imperial civil examinations at the highest level, 34 successful candidates of the imperial civil examinations at the highest level, and 78 at the provincial level, creating glorious miracles in the civilization of the culture of farming and studying. The Song Dynasty witnessed exceptional emergences of talents, with five successful candidates of the imperial civil examinations at the highest level at the same time. At present, there is no trace of the Wugui (Five Laurels) Memorial Arch which commemorated the "Five Sons Who Passed the Imperial Civil Examination," but the Zhuangyuan (Top Successful Scholar of the Imperial Civil Examination at the Highest Level) Building, built in the Southern Song Dynasty, still stands towering and bears witness to the prosperity of the Dong Clan with multiple successful candidates of the imperial civil examination at the highest level and cloudlike officials. During the Ming and Qing dynasties the people of Liukeng became rich with the bamboo and wood trade, leaving behind numerous beautiful buildings and other cultural relics. Liukeng features great natural attractions. It is worthy of its reputation as the "First Village for All Eternity" for its prosperity in the imperial civil examinations, the large number of officials, the wealth of its merchants, the size of its clans, and the duration of its history.

15 理坑：山中邹鲁，理学渊源
Likeng: Mountainous Land like 'the Hometowns of Confucius and Mencius' and the Place of Origin for Neo-Confucianism

江西婺源理坑村，始建于北宋末年，为余姓聚居地。古村三面环山，因理源溪抱村而过，得名"理源"，俗称"理坑"。婺源是理学家朱熹的故乡，理坑深受程朱理学熏陶，是真正的诗书之乡，出过学者近百人，著作近六百卷，其中有七十八卷入选《四库全书》，村口理源桥上所刻"山中邹鲁，理学渊源"，其言不虚。"学而优则仕"，村中曾有七品以上官宦三十六人，为后人留下了丰富精彩的明清官邸群。现存的一百二十余幢官邸气势不凡、各具特色，其中尤以明代吏部尚书余懋衡的"天官上卿"府、明代知府余自怡的驾睦堂、清代司马余维枢的司马第和清代光禄大夫余启官的云溪别墅最值得一观。这些古建或质朴高雅，或精美绝伦，或棱角分明，或外圆内方，透露出主人不同的人生信念和审美意趣，可堪玩味。

Located in Wuyuan, Jiangxi Province, Likeng Village was first built as a settlement for the people surnamed Yu in the late Northern Song Dynasty (960–1127). The ancient village is surrounded by mountains on three sides. It is named "Liyuan" or commonly known as "Likeng" because of the Liyuan Stream that flows through the village. Wuyuan is the hometown of Zhu Xi (1130–1200), a Neo-Confucian scholar. Under the in-depth influence of Neo-Confucianism, Likeng is truly a cultural town, with nearly one hundred scholars and nearly six hundred volumes of writings, of which seventy-eight volumes were selected into the *Siku Quanshu* (a collection of books compiled during the Qing Dynasty). On the Liyuan Bridge at the entrance of the village are inscriptions which read "A Mountainous Land Like the Hometowns of Confucius and Mencius and the Place of Origin for Neo-Confucianism," which are not exaggerated. There's a saying that "a good scholar will make an official." The village witnessed the emergence of 36 officials of the seventh grade and above, leaving a rich and wonderful collection of official residences of the Ming and Qing dynasties for future generations. There are over 120 official residences, each with its own distinctive features, among which the Tianguan Shangqing (Heavenly Official and Senior Minister) Mansion of Yu Maoheng (around 1607), the Minister of Appointments in the Ming Dynasty; the Jiamu Hall of Yu Ziyi (1594–1639), a governor of the Ming Dynasty; the Minister's Residence of Yu Weishu (1613–1667), a minister of the Qing Dynasty; and the Yunxi (Cloud and Stream) Villa of Yu Qiguan (around the 19th century), the Glorious Grand Master of the Qing Dynasty are most worth visiting. These ancient buildings are either rustic and elegant, or exceptionally exquisite, or of angular or rounded shapes, revealing the different beliefs and aesthetic interests of their owners. They are worth appreciating.

16 上清：道教福地，南国仙都
Shangqing: Blessed Land of Taoism and Fairy Capital of the South

上清镇坐落于江西鹰潭市龙虎山东侧的河谷盆地中，芦溪河环抱古镇，潆洄西流。东汉时，道教祖师张道陵至此开宗演法、修道大成。上清的地位从这一刻起被历史定格，此后历代天师世居此地，天师府被称作道教祖庭，龙虎山被誉为道教第一仙境。步入天师府，只见重檐丹楹、碧瓦朱扉，豫樟成林、浓荫散绿，一派仙气中万象庄严，真不负"仙都"之誉。自天师府东行二里，便是上清宫。此地风水绝佳，既是历代天师阐教演法、传度授箓的道场，也是供祀神仙、修真养性的宝地。昔日廊腰缦回、檐牙高啄的巍峨殿宇，如今遍地衰草枯杨，唯余一井。这口井，就是造就水浒传奇的镇妖井。凑近苔痕斑驳的井台，想象那三十六天罡、七十二地煞是如何化为一股黑烟，从井口蹿将出去，旋即散作百十道金光，变成一百零八将淆乱乾坤，演绎一曲惊天动地的英雄悲歌。

Shangqing Town is located in a river valley basin on the eastern side of the Longhu (Dragons and Tigers) Mountain in Yingtan City, Jiangxi Province. The ancient town is surrounded by the Luxi River which flows gently to the west. In the Eastern Han Dynasty (25–220), Zhang Daoling (34–156), the founder of Taoism, came here to establish a religion, expound on the religious principles, cultivate the Tao, and make great achievements. From this moment onwards, the status of Shangqing was fixed in history. Since then, generations of celestial masters in Taoism have lived here. The Celestial Master's Mansion has been called the ancestral temple of Taoism, while the Longhu Mountain has been hailed as the first fairyland of Taoism. Stepping into the Celestial Master's Palace, you will see the overlapping eaves, crimson pillars, blue tiles, and vermilion gate. Under the forests of camphor trees offering shade and green sights, you will drink in its majestic look which lives up to the reputation of the "immortal capital". Two li eastward from the Celestial Master's Palace is the Shangqing (Upper Clarity) Palace. It is a place of exceptional Fengshui geomantic omen, being the Taoist venue for celestial masters of different eras to preach on the religious doctrine, have ordination ceremonies, and impart Taoist written charms, and being a venue for worshipping deities, cultivating perfection, and nourishing the inner nature. The majestic building with winding corridors and overhanging eaves has been reduced to a well on dry land with withered plants. It is the well of demon suppression that gave rise to the legendary ancient Chinese novel *Outlaws of the Marsh*. Approaching the mossy well platform, you can imagine how the 36 stars of heavenly spirits and 72 stars of earthly fiends changed into a stream of black smoke, leaped out of the well, scattered into over one hundred golden lights, turned into 108 generals who wreaked havoc in the world, and performed an earth-shaking heroic elegy.

第三章
Chapter 3

彩云之南
Yunnan — South of the Colorful Clouds

大理：苍洱毓秀，风花雪月
Dali: Well-Endowed Cang'er amid Romantic Themes

　　大理是许多人心中的"诗和远方"。第一次到大理的人，会惊叹于这里绝美的云，离得那样近，仿佛触手可及。大理古城在滇西，东临水天一色的洱海，西枕终年叠翠的苍山，家家鲜花萦绕，户户清泉淙淙，如斯美景已经留驻千年。早在三千多年前，洱海周围就居住着白族先民，唐宋时期先后建都于此的南诏国、大理国等地方政权延续了五百余年，后归于中央统。现在的大理古城是明朝初年在旧城基础上修筑的，城楼巍峨，街巷棋盘式格局，人民路横贯古城南北。走在人民路上，往下看是洱海的幽蓝，举头望是苍山的积雪，路旁白墙青瓦，行人如在画中。大理古建很多，不必说著名的崇圣寺三塔和文献楼，仅是城中那一幢幢飞檐翘角、配色清雅的传统白族民居就令人心折。那"三坊一照壁"的结构、层次分明的漏透雕、斗拱彩画的辉煌门楼，散发着独有的白家魅力。

Dali is a place of "poetry and dreaming lands" for many people. Those who visit Dali for the first time will marvel at the exceptionally beautiful clouds that are so close as if they are within reach. Located in the west of Yunnan, Dali Ancient Town is bordered by the Erhai Lake where the sky and water merge in one color in the east and the Cangshan Mountain which remains green all the year long in the west. Here, every house is adorned by blooming flowers and murmuring springs, where such a beautiful landscape has lasted for millennia. As early as 3,000 years ago, the area around the Erhai Lake was inhabited by the ancestors of the Bai ethnic group. In the Tang and Song dynasties, local regimes such as Nanzhao state (738-902) and Dali state (937–1094, 109–1253), which had their capitals here, continued for more than 500 years before coming under the unified rule of the central government. The present Dali Ancient Town was built in the early Ming Dynasty on the basis of the old city, with lofty gate towers, a chessboard pattern of streets and alleys, and the People's Road running north and south through the ancient city. On the People's Road, you can look down at the tranquil blue of the Erhai Lake and up at the snow mantle of the Cangshan Mountain. You can also see white walls and green tiles by the roadside and pedestrians sauntering as if in a painting. Dali abounds in ancient buildings. Not to mention the famous Three Pagodas of the Chongsheng Temple and the Literature Pagoda, the traditional residential buildings of the Bai ethnic group in the city with overhanging eaves and cornices and elegant colors are overwhelmingly fascinating. Such elements, including the structure of the "one screen wall with three sides of living quarters," the well-layered fretwork, and the splendid arches with painted *Donggong* (corbel brackets), reveal the unique charm of families of the Bai ethnic group.

双廊：南诏风情，水天一色
Shuanglang: Nanzhao's Local Conditions and Customs amid Natural Sceneries Featuring the Sky and Water Merging into One Color

人言道：大理风光在苍洱，苍洱风光在双廊。双廊位于大理市东北端，三面环山，西临洱海，是一座有千年历史的白族渔村古镇。古镇北有萝莳曲，南有莲花曲，前有金梭、玉几双岛环抱于双曲间，故得名"双廊"。唐宋时期这里是南诏国、大理国的水军基地，也曾是悲风猎猎的古战场，而今古炮台遗址成了玉几岛上远眺苍山十九峰的最佳处。在玉几岛最临水端依崖而建的，是舞蹈家杨丽萍的太阳宫和月亮宫。山水与艺术，在此绝妙融合。悠久的历史和遗世独立的地理环境，给双廊留下了丰富的文化古迹和明清白族民居。泛舟洱海，登上著名的南诏风情岛，一尊巍峨的汉白玉观音雕像即刻映入眼帘。这尊雕像高十八米，是根据大理国时存留下来的阿嵯耶观音造像所雕绘，意态安详，水天一色中有说不出的震撼，见之忘俗。

It is said that the scenery of Dali is in Cang'er while the scenery of Cang'er is in Shuanglang. Located at the north-eastern end of Dali City, Shuanglang is surrounded by mountains on three sides and the Erhai Lake to its west. It is an ancient fishing town with a history of millennia in the Bai ethnic group. The town has Luoshiqu in its north, Lianhuaqu in its south, and Jinshuo and Yuji Islands in its front and between Luoshiqu and Lianhuaqu. As a result, it is named Shuanglang (Double Corridors). During the Tang and Song dynasties, it was a base for the naval forces of the Nanzhao and Dali kingdoms, and an ancient battlefield with the howling baleful sound of the wind. At present, the ruins of the ancient fortress are the best places to see in the distance the 19 peaks of Cangshan Mountain from Yuji Island. At the most waterfront end of the Yuji Island, built on the cliff are the Taiyang (Sun) Palace and Yueliang (Moon) Palace of Yang Liping (1958–, a Chinese dancer). The landscape and art have blended wonderfully here. The time-honored history and secluded geography have made Shuanglang rich in cultural monuments and residential buildings of the Bai ethnic group of the Ming and Qing dynasties. You can also go boating on the Erhai Lake and set foot on the famous Nanzhao Fengqing (Customs) Island, where you can admire the majestic Chinese marble statue of Avalokiteśvara. The statue, which is 18 meters high, is based on a statue of Avalokiteśvara that survives from the Dali kingdom period (937–1253). Its serene posture amid the water and sky merging into one color is indescribably striking and transcendental.

03 沙溪：茶马古道，千年集市
Shaxi: Ancient Tea-Horse Road and Millennium-old Market

云南剑川县沙溪古镇，坐落于"三江并流"世界自然遗产保护区东南部，自古是茶马古道上的交通要冲，马蹄声中曾繁华千载。古镇中心的寺登街是贸易往来集散地，过去每天有成千上万的马帮熙来攘往喧腾入云，如今一切归于寂静，古道、古宅、老马店……几乎都完好地矗立原地，这里成了茶马古道上唯一幸存的古集市。走到四方街上，目光立刻被东侧那座飞檐叠角的古戏台所吸引。这座清代戏台为三重檐魁阁式，前台后阁、结构巧妙，雕绘精妙立体，散发着令人沉迷的神秘美感。四方街西侧的兴教寺是国内仅存的明代白族阿吒力佛教寺院。庙宇大殿采用典型的藏传佛教周庑式建筑，二殿采用的是佛教密宗式建筑，独特的格局反映了沙溪多民族宗教历史文化的融合。走进清末马帮马锅头留下的欧阳大院，轩敞弘阔，满眼是精巧灵动的剑川木雕，诉说着当年马帮文化的兴旺发达。

Shaxi Ancient Town, which is located in Jianchuan County of Yunnan Province, sits in the southeast of the Three Parallel Rivers of World Natural Heritage Sites. It has been a major traffic hub on the Ancient Tea-Horse Road since ancient times, enjoying prosperity for millennia amid hoofbeats. Sideng Street, which is the ancient town's center, was a trading hub. In the past, thousands of cargo-horse caravans bustled around every day, but now everything has returned to silence. Ancient roads, ancient buildings, ancient inns for cargo-horse caravans... are almost intact in the places where they have been. This is the only surviving ancient market of the Ancient Tea-Horse Road. Walking on Sifang (Four Directions) Street, your eyes are immediately drawn to the ancient theater with its overhanging eaves and cornices on the east side. Built in the Qing Dynasty, the theatre is in the style of a towering pavilion with triple eaves. With its ingenious structure with a terrace in the front and a pavilion at the back and its delicate and three-dimensional carving and painting technique, it has exuded an enchanting and mysterious beauty. The Xingjiao Temple on the west side of Sifang Street is the only remaining Acharya Buddhist monastery of the Bai ethnic group from the Ming Dynasty in China. The Main Hall of the temple is built in the typical Tibetan Buddhist *Wudian* roof (Chinese hipped roof) style, while the Second Hall is built in the Tantric Buddhist style. Its unique pattern reflects the fusion of Shaxi's multi-ethnic religious history and culture. Entering the spacious and wide Ouyang Compound left behind by the leaders of cargo-horse caravans of the late Qing Dynasty, you will have a visual feast of the exquisite and dynamic Jianchuan wood carvings which tell about the prosperity of the culture of cargo-horse caravans back then.

凤羽：百鸟朝凤，文武有道
Fengyu: All birds Paying Homage to the Phoenix and a Land with Well-Balanced Cultural and Martial Achievements

在洱海源头、苍山云弄峰北麓，有一座美丽千年的白族古镇凤羽。镇西的鸟吊山是候鸟南迁的中转站，每年仲秋时节，万千候鸟云集于此，形成"百鸟朝凤"的自然奇观。凤羽曾是茶马古道上的重要驿站和马帮据点，鸟吊山是古道上最险峻的一段。昔年的热闹喧嚣早已随古道的衰落湮灭于岁月之中，那些年代久远的精美古建却得以完好留存。走在凤羽幽深的古巷中，一不小心就迷失在那六百余座明清白族民居院落中。那一幢幢"三坊一照壁"的四合院落，还有那"四合五天井"甚至"六合同春"的套院中，门楼飞檐叠角，照壁、横披、板裙、耍头、吊柱、栏杆……处处精雕细绘，色彩清雅，令人目不暇接。凤羽是文墨之乡，虽远在边陲却人才辈出，文武皆出过举人。文庙清绝的书法、武庙雄浑的大刀，记载着古镇灿烂的文明。

At the source of the Erhai Lake and the northern foot of the Yunnong (Frolicking Clouds) Peak in the Cangshan Mountain, there is the beautiful and millennium-old Fengyu Ancient Town of the Bai ethnic group. The Niaodiao Mountain in the west of the town is a stopover for migratory birds migrating southward. In mid-autumn every year, thousands of migratory birds gather here, creating a natural spectacle of "all birds paying homage to the phoenix". Fengyu was once an important post station and a stronghold for cargo-horse caravans on the Ancient Tea-Horse Road. The Niaodiao Mountain is the most precipitous section of the ancient road. While the hustle and bustle of the past have been lost to the ages with the decline of the ancient road, the exquisite ancient buildings of the past have survived and remained intact. Walking through the deep ancient alleys of Fengyu, you will find it easy to get lost in the courtyards of more than six hundred residential buildings of the Bai ethnic group in the Ming and Qing dynasties. In the quadrangle courtyards of the "one screen wall with three sides of living quarters," and the suite courtyards of "a quadrangle courtyard with five patios" and even of "a hexagonal courtyard sharing spring scenery". The gate towers feature overhanging eaves and cornices. Such spots as the screen walls, horizontal wall inscriptions, skirting boards, *Shuatou* (a part of *Dougong*, corbel brackets), hanging trusses, balustrades, and others are exquisitely carved and meticulously painted with fresh and elegant colors, presenting an overwhelming visual feast. Fengyu is a home of cultural studies. Although it is far away from the frontier, it witnessed the emergence of talents in large numbers, having produced successful candidates of the imperial civil examination at the provincial level. The clear and exceptional calligraphy of the Confucian Temple and the majestic broadsword of the Temple to the God of War record the splendid civilization of the ancient town.

05 大研：丽江王城，古乐悠长
Dayan: The Royal City of Dali with Lingering Ancient Music

　　大研镇坐落于滇西北丽江坝中部，北靠象山，西依狮子山，远处有玉龙雪山映照。从象山山麓流出的玉泉水分成无数支流穿行于古镇街巷，正所谓"家家门前活流水，户户垂杨拂屋檐。粉团花红引蝶来，雪山倒影映溪面"。环境得天独厚的大研镇是丽江古城所在地，古城始建于宋末元初，历经千载，这里的建筑融合了汉、白、彝、藏、纳西族等各民族的精华，至今格局如旧，大量古建存留完好，行走其间有穿越之感。1997年丽江古城被列入世界遗产名录。在《鹿鼎记》中多次出场的木王府，就在大研。它是明代木氏土司的"王宫"，建筑恢宏大气、雕饰精美绝伦，有"丽江紫禁城"之称。在古城能看到纳西族独有的"东巴文"，这是世界上唯一活着的图画象形文字；还能听到传承千年的纳西古乐，那深沉辉煌又柔和悦耳的古韵，超越时空，沁入灵魂深处。

　　Dayan Town is situated in the middle of Lijiang Dam in northwest Yunnan, with Xiangshan (Elephant) Mountain to the north, Shizi (Lion) Mountain to the west, and Yulong (Jade Dragon) Snow Mountain in the distance. The jade-like spring water flowing from the foot of the Xiangshan Mountain is divided into countless tributaries to flow through the streets and alleys of the ancient town, as a poem goes: "Every family has a living stream before its door. Every household has a poplar caressing its eaves. The pink clusters of red flowers attract butterflies. The snow-capped mountain is reflected on the stream's surface." Dayan Town, with exceptionally good geographical conditions, is the site of the Lijiang Ancient Town. Built in the late Song (960–1279) and early Yuan (1271–1368) dynasties, it has a history of about one thousand years. Here, the buildings combine the essences of the Han, Bai, Yi, Tibetan, Naxi, and other ethnic groups. With its pattern as before, it has preserved a large number of ancient buildings. You seem to be traveling through time and space to walk among them. The Lijiang Ancient Town was inscribed on the World Heritage List in 1997. The Mu King's Mansion, which makes several appearances in the renowned martial arts novel *The Deer and*

the Cauldron, is in Dayan. It was the "royal palace" of the government-appointed hereditary tribal headman (the Mu Clan) in the Ming Dynasty. With magnificent buildings and exceptionally exquisite carvings, it has been known as the "Forbidden City of Lijiang". In the ancient town, you can see the unique Dongba script of the Naxi ethnic group, the world's only living pictorial hieroglyphics. Besides, you can hear the ancient music of the Naxi people, which has been handed down for millennia. With the deep, glorious, soft, and melodious antique appeal, it transcends time and space and penetrates souls.

束河：清泉之乡，雪山倒映
Shuhe: A Hometown of Clear Springs with Reflections of Snow-capped Mountains

　　束河距大研十余里，亦属丽江古城范围。这里是纳西族先民最早的聚居点，也是丽江木氏土司的发祥地。束河是茶马古道上重要的中转站和皮毛交易集散地，宋元已成集镇，明清更加繁盛。从滇南来的马帮踏过青龙桥，翻越雪山前需在此换乘耐寒的束河马，束河人制作的皮货、铜器等冠绝一时，被马帮带到了藏区或更遥远的地方。如今游人"闲乘月"的四方街，当年是商贾云集的繁华集市。从玉龙雪山蜿蜒而下的清泉，在镇北龙泉山下形成九鼎、束河两个龙潭，潭水清寒如玉，"游鱼皆若无所依"，水草曼舞、雪山倒映，清姿傲岸，恍若仙境。潭水分作三道流入古镇密如棋盘的水渠，使户户泉水淙淙。龙潭上端是始建于乾隆年间的三圣宫，殿中供奉着观音、龙王和皮匠祖师孙膑。对于旧时靠天吃饭、靠皮革致富的束河人来说，这三位大概是最值得尊崇的吧。

　　More than 10 li from Dayan, Shuhe is also within the boundaries of the Lijiang Ancient Town. This is the earliest settlement of the ancestor of the Naxi ethnic group and also the birthplace of the government-appointed hereditary tribal headman (the Mu Clan). Shuhe was a significant transit point and fur trading distribution center on the Ancient Tea-Horse Road. It became a market town during the Song and Yuan dynasties, and even more prosperous during the Ming and Qing dynasties. The cargo-horse caravans from southern Yunnan crossed the Qinglong Bridge and changed here for the cold-resistant Shuhe horses before crossing the snowy mountains. The leather goods and brassware made by the Shuhe people were the best for a time. They were taken by the cargo-horse caravans to Xizang or further lands. The Sifang (Four Directions) Street, where visitors now "enjoy in ease", was once a bustling marketplace for merchants back then. The clear spring meandering down from Yulong (Jade Dragon) Snow Mountain forms two dragon pools named Jiuding and Shuhe, at the foot of the Longquan (Dragon Spring) Mountain in the north of the town. The water is as cold as jade and "the fish are swimming as if without any support". The water and grass are dancing gracefully. Reflected by the water, the snow-capped mountains also show their clear postures on the banks, presenting a fairyland. The water flows in three channels into the dense chessboard-like ditches of the ancient town, making the water murmur before every household. At the upper end of the dragon pool is the Sansheng (Three Saints) Palace built during the reign of Emperor Qianlong and worshiping the Avalokiteśvara, the Dragon King, and Sun Bin (–316 BC, ancient Chinese political strategist) hailed as the ancestor of leatherworkers. These three are probably the most revered of all for the people of Shuhe, who lived at the mercy of the weather and relied on leather to amass wealth in the old days.

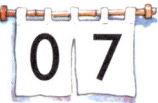

07 鲁史：茶叶之乡，马蹄铿锵

Lushi: A Hometown of Tea Leaves amid Clanging Hoofbeats

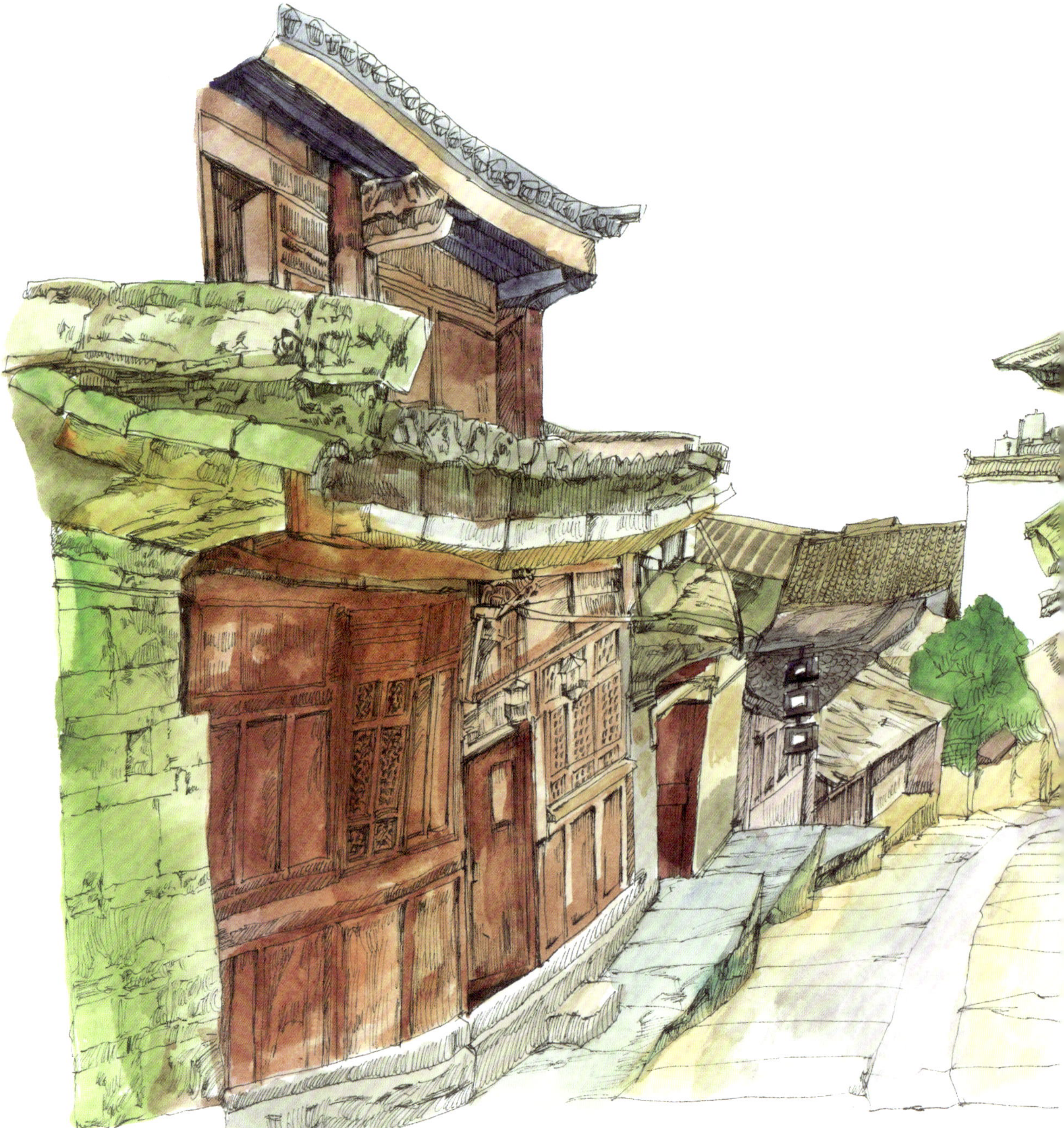

鲁史坐落于云南凤庆县的深山之中，前拥黑惠江、背靠澜沧江，地势险要，是茶马古道必经之地，也是滇西第一要塞古镇。鲁史古称"阿鲁司"，在彝语中意为"马帮经常出入的小镇"。从楼梯街走入古镇，脚下的石阶被时空打磨得光可鉴人，数百年间骡马踏出的一个个深坑烙印清晰可辨。驻足倾听，当年响彻古道的马铃声和清脆的马蹄声仿佛萦绕耳畔……漫步古镇，南诏、江浙、徽派等不同风格的古建民居错落有致，多个民族的建筑文化在此交融升华。楼梯街最陡处是骆家大院，四合院内走马转阁，气势壮观。宅院的主人是鲁史人工种茶第一人骆英才，他的俊昌号茶庄在民国曾盛极一时。今天四方街上的魁星阁、文昌宫、古戏楼都还在，只是不见当年集市的喧嚣繁华，只有兴隆寺外的古井还为鲁史人所用，取古井水，烹普洱茶，品人生百味。

Located in the deep mountains of Fengqing County in Yunnan Province, Lushi has the Heihui River in the front and the Lancang River on the back. With its steep and strategic terrain, it is the only way for the Ancient Tea-Horse Road and the first fortress town in western Yunnan. In ancient times, Lushi was called "Alusi," which means "a town frequented by cargo-horse caravans" in the language of the Yi ethnic group. As you walk down the stairway into the old town, you will see the stone steps brightly polished by the passage of time. The deep potholes made by pack animals over the centuries are clearly recognizable. If you stop to listen, you seem to take in the sounds of horse bells and the crisp hoofbeats that rang through the ancient roads... Strolling through the ancient town, you will see that ancient residential buildings of different styles such as of Nanzhao, Jiangzhe (Jiangsu and Zhejiang) and Huizhou are strewn about in attractive disorder, where the architectural cultures of many ethnic groups have mingled and sublimated. At the steepest point of Louti (Staircases) Street is the Luo's Family Compound, with a spatial and majestic quadrangle courtyard. The owner of the mansion is Luo Yingcai, the first person to grow tea artificially in Lushi, with his Junchang Tea Shop being a great fashion in the Republic of China. At present, the Kuixing Pavilion, the Wenchang (Cultural Prosperity) Palace, and the Ancient Theater on Sifang (Four Directions) Street are all still there, just without the hustle and bustle of the market back then. Only the ancient well outside the Xinglong (Prosperity) Temple is still used by the people of Lushi. They fetch the water from the ancient well, cook Pu'er tea, and taste all the flavors of life.

08 建水：滇南邹鲁，文献名邦
Jianshui: A Southern Yunnan Land like the Hometowns of Confucius and Mencius and a Famous Land of Literature

建水古城位于滇南红河州，唐代南诏政权在此筑惠历土城。"惠历"在古彝语中意为"大海"，汉语译作"建水"。明代朝廷在此设临安府，并"移中土大姓，以实云南"。无数中原和江南移民把丰富的汉文化带到了这座小城，他们按照传统的营造法式，在土城的基础上扩建砖城，建水今天的古城格局，就是当年的遗存。从东门进入古城，首先映入眼帘的是宏伟壮丽的朝阳楼，这座城楼历经六百余年风雨沧桑，始终巍然屹立，象征着建水边陲重镇的地位。登楼远眺，城中精雅古建绵延不绝。朱家花园内雅外秀、层次丰富，据说是仿《红楼梦》中园林所建，有"滇南大观园"之誉。建水的孔庙气象恢宏，规模仅次于曲阜孔庙。这与建水重文崇礼、尊师重道的风尚是分不开的。在明清的科举中榜者中，临安府能占到云南半数左右，是名副其实的"滇南邹鲁，文献名邦"。

Jianshui Ancient Town, which is located in Honghe Prefecture in southern Yunnan, was originated from the Huili Earthen City built by the Nanzhao regime in the Tang Dynasty. "Huili", which means the "sea" in the ancient language of the Yi ethnic group, is translated as "Jianshui" in Mandarin Chinese. During the Ming Dynasty, the imperial court set up the Lin'an Prefecture here and "moved renowned Chinese clans and families to enrich Yunnan". Numerous immigrants from the Central Plains and the south of the Yangtze River brought their rich Han culture to this small city. They built the brick city on top of the earthen one following traditional rules of architecture. The ancient town pattern of Jianshui seen today is a remnant of those days. Entering the ancient town through the East Gate, you will be first greeted with the magnificent Chaoyang (Sun-Facing) Tower, which has been towering through more than 600 years of vicissitudes, symbolizing the status of Jianshui as a major town on the frontier. A look into the distance from the tall tower reveals the exquisite and undulating ancient buildings in the city. The Zhu's Family Garden, with its elegant interior and beautiful exterior among balanced layers, is said to have been built in imitation of the gardens in the ancient Chinese novel *Dream of the Red Chamber*. It has been known as the "Grand View Garden of Southern Yunnan". Jianshui's Confucius Temple is magnificent, second in scale only to the Confucius Temple in Qufu, Shandong Province. This is inseparable from Jianshui's trend of valuing literature and rituals, respecting teachers, and revering teaching. In the Ming and Qing dynasties, Lin'an Prefecture accounted for about half of the successful candidates in the imperial civil examinations, enabling it to truly be "A Southern Yunnan Land like the Hometowns of Confucius and Mencius and a Famous Land of Literature".

09 和顺：滇南侨乡，绝胜苏杭
Heshun: An Overseas Chinese Hometown in Southern Yunnan, with Its Landscape Better than those in Suzhou and Hangzhou

和顺古镇位于云南"极边之城"腾冲境内，四面火山环抱，一泓碧水绕村。这里曾是马帮重镇、南方丝绸之路的必经之地。四百多年前，和顺人就开始"走夷方"，去缅甸、印度或更远的地方经商。衣锦还乡之时，他们也把海外文化带回了故土。古镇始建于明初，朱元璋的屯边令把许多中原、江南、四川移民汇聚于此，汉文化从此在这里落地生根。走入古镇，有八座风格各异的华美宗祠，有儒释道三教合一的明代道观……千余幢传统民居中，以粉墙黛瓦的徽派风格为主，也可见"三坊一照壁"的南诏风格、西洋建筑元素以及四合院等。六百多年来，中原文化、侨乡文化、南诏文化、边地文化在此交融共生，形成和顺独有的人文底蕴。和顺还拥有我国创立最早、规模最大的乡间图书馆，馆名为胡适所题，现有藏书七万余册，是名副其实的"书香名里"。

Heshun Ancient Town is located in Tengchong, which is hailed as "a city of the extreme border" in Yunnan, and surrounded by volcanoes on all sides and a vast expanse of green water. It was once a major town for cargo-horse caravans and the only way on the Southern Silk Road. Over 400 years ago, the people of Heshun began to travel to alien lands, making way to Myanmar, India, and further destinations to do business. When they returned home, they also brought overseas cultures back to their homeland. The ancient town was built in the early Ming Dynasty, when Emperor Hongwu (r. 1368–1398) issued orders to send garrison troops or peasants to open up wasteland and grow grain in the border areas, bringing many immigrants from the Central Plains, the south of the Yangtze River, and Sichuan to this place. As a result, the Han culture took root here. Walking into the ancient town, you will see eight magnificent ancestral temples in different styles and Taoist temples that unite Confucianism, Buddhism, and Taoism in the Ming Dynasty... More than 1,000 traditional residential buildings are mostly of the Huizhou style with white walls and grey tiles. You can lay eyes on the Nanzhao style of "one screen wall with three sides of living quarters," western architectural elements, quadrangle courtyards, among others. For over 600 years, the cultures of the Central Plains, of the hometown of overseas Chinese, of Nanzhao, and of the borderlands have mingled and coexisted here, forming a unique cultural heritage for Heshun. Heshun also has the earliest and largest rural library in China, with its name inscribed by Hu Shi (1891–1962, a Chinese scholar). It has a collection of over 70,000 books. It is a genuine "famous town of literary reputation".

黑井：千年盐都，灵源普泽
Heijing: A Millennium-old Salt Capital with a Spiritual Source and Widespread Benefits

黑井古镇坐落于云南楚雄的"恐龙之乡"禄丰县玉碧山脚下，龙川江的河谷之中。黑井历史悠久，三千多年前就有彝族先民在此生息。这里自古产盐，南诏大理时期黑井盐成为专供王室的贡盐，明清时期黑井盐业臻于鼎盛，黑井盐税占到云南盐税的六成以上。近代由于海盐的引入，这座千年盐都走向衰落，盐文化和历代古建却流传下来。气势雄伟的武家大院，见证着昔日盐业的无限繁荣。走进这座清代著名盐商武维扬的宅第，规模宏大、构思精巧。大院背山面水，呈"王"字形，纵一横三，有四个天井九十九间房一百零八扇门，暗含"六位高升、四通八达、九九通久、王隐其中"的深意。登楼远眺，古镇四街十八巷尽收眼底，节孝总坊、文庙、诸天寺等明清建筑古色古香。"以盐为礼"的习俗和以"盐焖鸡"为代表的盐焖美食，是古镇悠久盐文化的余韵遗响。

Heijing Ancient Town is located in the valley of the Longchuan River at the foot of the Yubi Mountain in Lufeng County. It is the "hometown of dinosaurs" in Chuxiong, Yunnan. Heijing features a time-honored history, with the ancestors of the Yi ethnic group living and working here over 3,000 years ago. Salt has been produced here since ancient times. During the Nanzhao Dali period (937–1254), Heijing salt became a tribute to the imperial family. During the Ming and Qing dynasties, Heijing's salt business reached its peak, accounting for over 60% of Yunnan's salt tax. As sea salt has been introduced in modern times, this millennium-old salt capital declined, but its salt culture and ancient buildings of the past eras have been passed down to the present day. The majestic Wu Family Compound bears witness to the unlimited prosperity of the salt business in the past. Entering the mansion of Wu Weiyang, a famous salt merchant of the Qing Dynasty, you will marvel at its grandeur and exquisite composition. The courtyard has mountains at its back and waters in its front. With one vertical and three horizontal lines (in the shape of *Wang*, the Chinese character of "king") in its layout, it has four patios, with 99 rooms and 108 doors, implying the deep connotations of "ascension for all six categories of sentient beings, accessibility from all sides, ever-lasting existence, and reclusiveness of a king-like figure." From the top of the building, you will have a panoramic view of the four streets and eighteen lanes of the ancient town and drink in the antique appeal of the Jiexiao Zongfang (General Memorial Arch of Integrity and Filial Piety), the Confucius Temple, the Zhutian (Heavenly Beings) Temple, and other buildings from the Ming and Qing Dynasty. The custom of "taking salt as a gift" and the salt casserole cuisine represented by the "salt chicken in a casserole" are the lingering appeal of the ancient town's time-honored salt culture.

第四章
Chapter 4

巴山蜀水
Mountains and Rivers in Sichuan

四川
Sichuan

01 阆中：阆苑仙境，巴蜀要冲
Langzhong: Fairyland Dwelled by Immortals and Strategic Location of Sichuan

阆中地处四川盆地东北缘、嘉陵江的中游，古城严格按照唐朝风水理论布局于山环水绕的形胜之地，棋盘式街巷中有五分之一仍保留着唐宋时的格局，明清建筑鳞次栉比，民居融合南北精华而独具神韵，是我国保存最完整的风水古城。因是巴蜀要冲，三国名将张飞曾于此镇守七年，精美恢宏的汉桓侯祠承载着阆中人对他的怀念。阆中是四川的状元之乡，明代的贡院、清代的考棚，见证着阆中昔日科举之盛。登上临江的华光楼，山光水色尽收眼底。城南的锦屏山，是画圣吴道子所绘《嘉陵江山图》的轴心，风景殊胜，素有"阆苑仙境"之誉；城北的玉台山上，唐朝的滕王阁辉煌巍峨，"清江锦石伤心丽，嫩蕊浓花满目斑"，是诗圣杜甫于此留下的千古名句。

Langzhong is located at the north-eastern edge of the Sichuan Basin and in the middle reaches of the Jialing River. The ancient town is laid out in a beautiful land surrounded by mountains and waters in strict accordance with the Fengshui geomantic omen theory of the Tang Dynasty. One-fifth of the chessboard-shaped streets still retain the pattern of the Tang and Song dynasties, with rows of buildings of the Ming and Qing dynasties. The residential buildings, which combine the essence of the north and the south, feature unique appeal. All these have made Langzhong the best-preserved ancient town with Fengshui geomantic omen in China. As Langzhou was a strategic location of Sichuan, Zhang Fei (168–221, also known as Duke Heng of the Han Dynasty), a famous general of the Three Kingdoms period (220–280), safeguarded this place for seven years. The magnificent and grand Temple of Duke Heng of the Han Dynasty carries the memory of the Langzhong people for him. Langzhong is the hometown of the top successful candidates of the imperial civil examinations of the highest level in Sichuan. It also housed the provincial imperial civil examination center in the Ming Dynasty and the imperial civil examination venue in the Qing Dynasty, thus bearing witness to the former prosperity of the imperial civil examinations in Langzhong. After climbing up to the Huaguang (Resplendent Light) Tower on the riverfront, you will have a panoramic view of the mountains and waters. To the south of the city is the Jinping (Brocade Screen) Mountain, the center of the *Painting of the Jialing River and Mountains* by Wu Daozi (686–760), who was hailed as the sage of painting. With exceptional scenery, it has been known as the "Fairyland for Immortals". To the north of the city is the Yutai (Jade Terrace) Hill, with the Tengwang (Prince Teng) Pavilion of the Tang Dynasty towering in all its splendor. "The clear water and the brocade-like rocks are beautiful but sorrow-provoking. New tender stamens and thickly colored flowers fill the eyes," was written by Du Fu (712–770) who was hailed as the sage of poetry in his well-known saying that has gone down in history.

02 丹巴藏寨：千碉之国，美人如玉
Danba Tibetan Villages: Land of Thousands of Watchtowers and Jade-Like Beauties

在川西高原横断山脉的峡谷之中，大渡河奔腾不息，大小金川汩汩交汇。在依山傍水的向阳坡梁上，丹巴的藏寨和碉楼随山势高低错落，与葱郁树林、清澈溪流、皑皑雪峰一起构成了绝美的嘉绒藏区风情画卷。从先秦古羌到汉代东女国，从唐代西山八国到乾隆平定大小金川，一座座岿然屹立的古朴碉楼，见证了丹巴走过的千年沧桑。外墙洁白如雪、绘饰明艳庄重的梯形藏寨耸立于春夏碧绿、秋季多彩的山林间，有惊世之美。丹巴有三绝，除了藏寨和碉楼群，还有一绝是美女。在墨尔多神山与邛山之间，藏着神秘的美人谷。相传千年前有一只凤凰飞到神山，后来幻化成万千美人，从此这里世代美女如云。大约是丹巴的灵山秀水养育了太多美丽的藏族姑娘，所以才有了这个美丽传说。

In the gorges of the Hengduan Mountains on the Western Sichuan Plateau, the Dadu River rushes on, with its branches gurgling and converging in Daxiaojinchuan. On the sunny slopes with mountains on one side and waters on the other, the Tibetan villages and watchtowers of Danba are in attractive disorder following the mountain features. With lush woods, clear streams, and snow-capped peaks, they form a beautiful picture of the local conditions and customs of the Jiarong Tibetan region. From the ancient Qiang in the pre-Qin Dynasty (before 221 BC) to the Dongnv Kingdom of the Han Dynasty (202 BC–220 AD), from the Eight Kingdoms of Xishan in the Tang Dynasty to the pacification of Daxiaojinchuan by Emperor Qianlong, the majestic ancient watchtowers witnessed that the Danba has gone through one thousand years of vicissitudes. Featuring snow-white walls and brightly painted decorations, the stately and terraced Tibetan villages stand amid the mountains which are green in spring and summer and colorful in autumn. They are of astonishing beauty. In addition to the Xizang villages and watchtowers, Danba's rarities include beauties. Between Murdo Holy Mountain and Qiongshan Mountain lies the mysterious Valley of Beauty. According to legend, a phoenix flew to the Holy Mountain one thousand years ago and later transformed into thousands of beauties. Since then the place has abounded in beauties for generations. The beautiful legend is probably because the beautiful mountains and waters of Danba have nurtured so many beautiful Xizang girls.

03 李庄：长江重镇，人文荟萃
Lizhuang: Strategic Town Along the Yangtze River with Rich Cultural Heritage

李庄坐落于川南宜宾市东郊长江南岸，此地"峰排桂岭，秀毓仙源"，有"万里长江第一镇"之称。走过一千四百余年的风雨沧桑，古镇仍保留着十八条明清街巷及众多古建民居，其中旋螺殿、奎星阁、九龙石碑、百鹤窗被建筑大师梁思成誉为"李庄四绝"。旋螺殿始建于明代，顶部藻井八面均用斗拱叠架成网目状花纹，从左至右盘旋而上，上下三层不用一钉却异常坚牢。其受力原理还被梁思成运用到了联合国大厦的顶部设计之中。1940年，同济大学、中央博物院、中国营造学社等十多所学府迁驻李庄，傅斯年、梁思成、林徽因、童第周等众多学者先后奔赴李庄，这座千年古镇以宽厚的胸膛庇护了颠沛流离中的文化精英，使他们的科研、创作和教学得以继续，使中国的科学和文化事业不至人才断层，这段同舟共济的历史值得后人永远铭记。

Lizhuang is located on the southern bank of the Yangtze River in the eastern suburbs of Yibin City in southern Sichuan. With its peaks surpassing those in Guilin and its beauty comparable to a fairyland, this land has been hailed as the first town along the Yangtze River. After over 1,400 years of vicissitudes, the town has maintained 18 streets and lanes and many ancient residential buildings of the Ming and Qing dynasties. Among them, the Xuanluo (Spiral Snail) Hall, the Kuixing (Great Bear Constellation) Pavilion, the Jiulong (Nine Dragons) Stone Monument, and the Baihe (One Hundred Cranes) Window were hailed by the architect Liang Sicheng (1901–1972) as the "Four Rarities of Lizhuang". The Xuanluo Hall was built in the Ming Dynasty. The eight sides of its caisson ceiling are turned into mesh-like patterns by using stacked *Dougong* (corbel brackets), which spiral upward from left to right, making the three-story structure exceptionally firm even without using a single nail. Its load-bearing principles were also applied by Liang Sicheng to the design of the top of the United

Nations Headquarters. In 1940, over a dozen institutions of learning, including Tongji University, the Central Museum (the present-day Nanjing Museum) and the Society for the Study of Chinese Architecture, moved to Lizhuang. Many scholars, such as Fu Sinian (1896–1950, a Chinese scholar), Liang Sicheng, Lin Huiyin (1904–1955, a Chinese architect) and Tong Dizhou (1902–1979, a Chinese biologist), made way to Lizhuang. This millennium-old town, with its inclusiveness, sheltered displaced cultural elites, allowing them to continue their scientific research, creation, and teaching, so that China's scientific and cultural endeavors had not suffered from a talent gap. This history of solidarity is worth remembering for generations to come.

尧坝：川黔走廊，伞韵涵芳
Yaoba: Sichuan-Guizhou Corridor, with Its Umbrellas Revealing Appeal and Fragrance

四川合江尧坝镇地处川黔结合部，北宋时辟为驿站，来往川南黔北间的马帮和商贩必经此地，商贸日盛，明清时期这里是川南最繁华的集镇。繁华逝去之后，明清风貌在这座偏僻小镇几乎没有改变，古街旁大多是典型的川南四合院民居。走入古镇，一座重檐四柱的高大石牌坊兀立眼前，这是嘉庆皇帝赐给剿匪灭患、为民除害的武进士李跃龙的。李跃龙的大鸿米店是古镇最有特色的建筑，也是当年川黔粮食贸易的重要集散地。黄健中的同名电影就是在这座精致典雅的两层四合院中拍摄的。这部电影也成就了尧坝古镇，此后郭宝昌、谢晋等名导纷至沓来，使这个本已淡出历史舞台的古镇，成了有名的川南影视城。古法制作的油纸伞，是古镇中最艳丽的风景。走入伞铺，红的是牡丹、白的是丁香，欢快的是喜鹊闹梅，幽静的是竹林听风……各式各样的油纸伞带来一场古典美学的视觉盛宴。

Located in Hejiang of Sichuan, Yaoba Town is at the junction of Sichuan and Guizhou. It was established as a post station during the Northern Song Dynasty. It was the only way for the cargo-horse caravans and merchants traveling between southern Sichuan and northern Guizhou. With its prospering trade, it became the most prosperous market town in southern Sichuan during the Ming and Qing dynasties. After its prosperity faded away, the conditions and customs of the Ming and Qing dynasties have barely changed in this remote town, with the ancient streets mostly lined with typical southern Sichuan quadrangle residential buildings. Entering the town, your eyes are greeted with a towering stone memorial arch with double eaves and four pillars. It was given by Emperor Jiaqing (r. 1796–1820) to Li Yuelong (around the 19th century), a successful candidate of the military imperial civil examination at the highest level and who fought against bandits and eliminated harm for the people. Li Yuelong's Dahong Rice Shop is the most distinctive building in the ancient town and was an important distribution center for the Sichuan-Guizhou grain trade back then. Huang Jianzhong's (1941–, a contemporary Chinese director) film of the same title was shot in this exquisite two-story quadrangle courtyard. The film also made Yaoba Ancient Town a sensation. Since then, Guo Baochang (born in 1940), Xie Jin (1923–2008), and other famous directors came in succession, making this ancient town, which had faded from the historical stage, a famous film and television town in southern Sichuan. The oil-paper umbrellas produced with time-honored methods are the most splendid sight in the ancient town. When you walk into an umbrella shop, you will see the red peonies, white lilacs, cheerful magpies frolicking on the plums, the quiet bamboo forests with caressing wind... A variety of oil-paper umbrellas bring a visual feast of classical aesthetics.

05 福宝：青山福地，天人合一
Fubao: Blessed Land amid Green Hills Featuring the Unity of Heaven and Humanity

合江福宝古镇位于川南边陲的大漕河畔，唐宋时为川黔茶马古道，明清时为川盐运往黔岸的必经之地。古镇依山而建，民居临水而筑，三水相汇，五桥相通，高低错落，曲折多姿。跨过回龙桥即入古镇，建于山脊的回龙古街蜿蜒于青瓦间隙，古街两侧明清吊脚楼顺山势起伏而下，看似摇摇欲坠，实则坚固无比。穿斗式木构架交错于洁白的编竹夹泥墙上，形成简洁而富于韵律的黑白方格图案。层次分明的山墙群是川南传统民居的经典符号，纵深构图完美如"一首空间的交响乐"。福宝古镇被誉为"中国山地民居建筑的精华"，三宫八庙是到此不可错过的古迹。这些经典民居大多保留完整、神韵犹存，其中建于明中期的清源宫名气最大，殿宇雕龙画凤、威严庄重。古镇还是国家级福宝森林公园的门户，高山密林中流瀑飞泉，生长于这样的山水格局中，福宝堪称天人合一的福地。

In Hejiang, Fubao is located on the banks of the Dacao River at the border area of southern Sichuan. It was a part of the Ancient Tea-Horse Road between Sichuan and Guizhou in the Tang and Song dynasties, and the only way for Sichuan salt to be transported to the Guizhou's territory in the Ming and Qing dynasties. The ancient town was built against the mountain, with residential buildings constructed facing the waters. With three rivers converging and five bridges connected, the ancient town features a variety of highs and lows as they are winding with varied and graceful appearances. After crossing the Huilong (Dragon-Returning) Bridge to enter the old town, you will see that the Huilong Street, built on the ridge of a hill, winding through the gaps in the green roof tiles. On both sides of the street, the houses supported by wooden pillars of the Ming and Qing dynasties were built following the mountain features. They seem shaky but are incredibly strong. The wooden frames of the crossed sets of brackets are interspersed on the white clay walls with woven bamboos, forming a simplistic and rhythmic black and white chevron pattern. The well-arranged gables are a classic symbol of traditional southern Sichuan residential buildings. The depth of the composition is perfect as a "symphony of space". Fubao Ancient Town is known as "the essence of Chinese mountainous residential buildings". The three palaces and eight temples are monuments not to be missed here. Most of these classic residential buildings have been well preserved with their appeal. Among them, the most famous one is the Qingyuan (Clear Source) Palace built in the mid-Ming Dynasty, with its carved and painted halls with dragon and phoenix patterns and its majestic and solemn ambiance. The ancient town is also the gateway to the national Fubao Forest Park, where waterfalls and springs flow from high mountains and dense forests. In such a landscape pattern, Fubao can be hailed as a blessed land featuring the unity of Heaven and humanity.

06 洛带：客家名镇，会馆之乡
Luodai: Famous Hakka Town and Hometown of Guilds

洛带古镇坐落于成都市龙泉山麓，始建于三国蜀汉时期，相传因蜀汉后主刘禅的玉带落入镇旁的八角井而得名"落带"，后雅称"洛带"。明末清初"湖广填四川"的移民运动，使大量客家人入川落籍。洛带是成都东山客家人聚居之地，至今仍保留着客家的乡音乡俗、乡韵乡貌，人称"西部客家第一镇"。今天洛带的千年老街仍保留着明清格局和建筑风貌，广东、江西、湖广、川北四大客家会馆坐落其间。客家会馆大多以中轴线对称布局，坐北朝南，寓意无限思乡之情。每个会馆各具地域风格，广东会馆殿宇嵯峨、气势宏伟，壮观的镬耳墙在四川绝无仅有，是洛带的地标建筑，也是全国保存最好的会馆之一。会馆是移民们的栖息地，是一部浓缩的移民史。徘徊其中，仿佛看到一代代客家人匆忙的身影，他们在这里交换着移民生活的喜与愁，寻求着乡情的归依和文化认同。

Located at the foot of Longquan (Dragon Spring) Mountain in Chengdu, Luodai Ancient Town was built during the Shu Han period (221–263) of the Three Kingdoms period. It is said to have been named "Luodai" (Fallen Belt) after the jade belt of Liu Shan (r. 233-263), the last king of the Shu Han Dynasty, fell into an octagonal well in the town. Later, it had an elegant name of "Luodai," where Luo is often used to refer to an honorific place name. In the late Ming and early Qing dynasties, a large number of Hakka people settled in Sichuan as a result of the migration movement of "filling Sichuan with the people from Hunan, Hubei, Guangdong, and Guangxi". Luodai is a place where the Hakka people live in Dongshan, Chengdu. Having preserved the Hakka accent, customs, appeal, and other features, it is known as the "first Hakka town in western China". At present, the millennium-old ancient street of Luodai still retains its pattern and architectural features of the Ming and Qing dynasties, accommodating four major Hakka guildhalls of Guangdong, Jiangxi, Huguang (Hunan, Hubei, Guangdong, and Guangxi) and northern Sichuan. Most of the Hakka guildhalls are symmetrically laid out along a central axis, facing north and south, thus signifying their infinite homesickness. Each guildhall has its own regional style. The Guangdong Guildhall features towering buildings amid its majestic ambiance, with its imposing wok-ear walls unfound in other places of Sichuan. As a landmark in Sichuan, it is one of the best-preserved guildhalls across China. Guildhalls, which are the habitats of the immigrants, represent a condensed history of immigration. Wandering around, you seem to be seeing generations of Hakka people bustling around, exchanging the joys and sorrows of migrant life, seeking dependence for homesickness and cultural identity.

07 罗泉：千年龙镇，保路救国
Luoquan: Millennium-old Dragon Town, Protecting the Roads and Saving the Country

　　罗泉地处四川资中、仁寿、威远三县交界的深丘中，古镇沿沱江支流珠溪河依势而建，一条五里长街蜿蜒曲折贯穿东西，形似蛟龙，因此罗泉有"川中第一龙镇"之誉。罗泉自秦朝起便是产盐基地，历经千年，至清中期达到顶峰。罗泉镇所产井盐在1925年获巴黎世界博览会金奖，品质冠绝天下。走过百年风雨的盐神庙，见证了罗泉盐业的盛衰兴废。庙中供奉的主位是盐神管仲，火神祝融和武圣关羽分立两侧。罗泉古街上有一处永载革命史册的重檐院落，1911年8月4日，罗泉井会议在此召开，随后发动的四川保路运动大大推动了辛亥革命的历史进程，四川人民的爱国抗争精神永垂青史。

　　Luoquan is located in the deep hills at the junction of Zizhong, Renshou, and Weiyuan counties in Sichuan. The ancient town was built along the Zhuxi River, a tributary of the Tuojiang River. A five-li-long street winds through the east and west of the ancient town, resembling a dragon, hence Luoquan's reputation as the "first dragon town in Sichuan". Luoquan has been a salt-producing base for millennia since the Qin Dynasty, reaching its peak in the mid-Qing Dynasty. The well salt produced in Luoquan, which won the gold medal at the Exposition Internationale des Arts Décoratifs et Industriels Modernes in 1925, features the highest quality in the world. The Yanshen (Salt God) Temple, which has endured centuries of vicissitudes, has seen the rises and falls of the Luoquan's salt business. The temple worships Guan Zhong (723–645 BC, ancient Chinese politician) as the God of Salt, with Zhu Rong (the God of Fire) and Guan Yu (the God of War) standing on either side. On Luoquan Ancient Street is a courtyard with double eaves that will forever be remembered in the books of revolutionary history. It was here that the Luoquanjing Conference was held on August 4, 1911, followed by the Sichuan Railway Protection Movement, which greatly contributed to the historical progress of the Xinhai Revolution in 1911 (which ended the feudal rule in China). The patriotic and struggling of the Sichuan people will go down in the annals of history.

08 仙市：盐道明珠，天上街市
Xianshi: Pearl on the Salt road and Market in Heaven

　　仙市原名仙滩，坐落于"千年盐都"自贡市东南的釜溪河畔，这里山形地貌宛若侧卧少女，相传玉帝之女曾陶醉于此间美景，下凡逍遥酣睡于河畔，故得名"仙滩"。古镇始建于隋、因盐而兴，曾是自贡井盐出川的第一个重要驿站和码头。如今一派宁静的釜溪河，当年帆樯如织、纤夫盈途，古镇上店铺林立、商贾云集，有"盐道明珠"之誉。如今古镇洗尽铅华，存留完好的明清建筑群默默讲述着繁华往事。南华宫和天上宫历经数百年风雨朱颜不改，依旧雕梁画栋气派非凡。金桥寺塔身佛光闪耀，幽谷梵音似清风萦怀。看过古风佛韵，还要尝一尝仙市地道的盐帮菜，品一品千年盐文化的真实滋味。

　　Xianshi was formerly known as Xiantan. It is located on the bank of the Fuxi River in the southeast of Zigong City known as the "Millennium-Old Salt Capital". Here, the mountainous terrain resembles a lying maiden. According to legend, the Jade Emperor's daughter was so enchanted by the beauty of this land that she descended on the world of mortals and slept soundly on the banks of the river, hence the name Xiantan (Fairy Beach). The ancient town was built in the Sui Dynasty (581-618). Prospered by salt, it was once the first important post station and wharf for Zigong's well salt to leave Sichuan. At present, the Fuxi River reveals a scenery of peace. Back then, the river was thronged with sails pulled by barge haulers in an endless stream on the road. In the ancient town, shops stood in great numbers while merchants gathered in crowds, earning it a reputation of "a pearl on the salt road". At present, the town has been washed off its excessive magnificence, with the surviving buildings of the Ming and Qing dynasties silently revealing stories of its prosperous past. The Nanhua (Southern Prosperity) Palace and the Tianshang (Heavenly) Palace have maintained their looks after undergoing vicissitudes of centuries, with their carved beams and painted rafters showcasing an extraordinary manner. The pagoda in the Jinqiao (Golden Bridge) Temple shines with the light of Buddha, while the Buddhist sounds from a tranquil valley seem to be a breeze soothing one's mind and body. After admiring the ancient customs and Buddhist appeal, you should try the authentic salt dishes of Xianshi and have a bite of the real taste of the millennium-old salt culture.

09

黄龙溪：天府仙境，火龙灯舞
Huanglongxi: Heavenly Fairy Land with Fire Dragons and Lantern Dances

黄龙溪位于成都双流区东南部，锦江与鹿溪一清一浊交汇于此，古人谓之"黄龙渡清江，真龙内中藏"，古镇由此得名"黄龙溪"。古镇有两千一百余年历史，古代是自成都南下的第一个码头，是"门泊东吴万里船"的头站。作为南方丝绸之路的货物集散地，黄龙溪曾有百货山积、帆樯如林的千年盛景。"日有千人拱手，夜有万盏明灯"，古人描绘码头重镇昔日繁华的辞章，如今依旧适用于游人如织的黄龙溪。古镇完好保留了明清鱼骨状街坊格局，七十六幢明清吊脚楼傍水而筑，体现了古蜀民居"干栏"文化特色。古龙寺、镇江寺、潮音寺皆坐落于正街上，形成了街中有庙、庙中有街的独特景观。源于南宋的"烧火龙"是古镇最驰名的民俗活动，2010年被列入国家非遗名录。每年正月，人们在溪水边舞动金龙穿梭于焰火中，水火相激、火花四溅，壮观瑰丽的景象令人一见难忘。

Huanglongxi is located in the southeast of Chengdu's Shuangliu District, where the Jinjiang River and the Lujiang Stream meet respectively as a clear and turbid river. As the ancients said that "With Huanglong (Yellow Dragon) crossing a clear river, a real dragon hides inside," thus giving the town its name "Huanglongxi" ("Yellow Dragon Stream"). The ancient town, which features a history of over 2,100 years, had the first dock to go southward from Chengdu in ancient times. it was the first stop mentioned in the poetic line that "Close by the gate are moored ships from the Wu land thousands of miles away." As a distribution center for goods on the Southern Silk Road, Huanglongxi witnessed the scenes of various goods stored like mountains and sails like forests for millennia. "In the daytime, thousands of people cup hands in greetings to each other; at night, thousands of lanterns are brightly lit." This poetic line depicting the former prosperity of the wharf in the strategic town still applies to Huanglongxi, a destination packed with tourists at present. The ancient town has well preserved its pattern of fishbone-like streets of the Ming and Qing dynasties, with seventy-six houses supported by pillars of the Ming and Qing dynasties built near the water, reflecting the cultural characteristics of the ancient Sichuan residential buildings featuring *Ganlan* (being supported by pillars). The Gulong (Ancient Dragon) Temple, Zhenjiang (River-Pacifying) Temple, and Chaoyin (Tide Sounds) Temple are all located on the main street, forming a unique landscape with temples and streets found in each other. Originating from the Southern Song Dynasty, the activity of "Burning the Dragon" is the most famous folklore activity in the ancient town. It was included in the National Intangible Cultural Heritage List in 2010. In the first month of each year, the people dance as they move the golden dragon through the fireworks by the stream. The spectacular sights of water and fire agitating each other and sparks flying about are truly unforgettable.

龙华：八仙立佛，凉桥卧波
Longhua: Standing Buddha Statues on the Eight Immortals Mountain and Cool Bridge Lying above the Waves

屏山县龙华古镇始建于宋代，明清时期形成现在的规模，是历代四川边防重镇。古镇负山襟水，发源于老君山的大小龙溪于此汇流，静卧溪上百年的靖虹桥古雅秀美，两岸古榕参天，炎夏立于桥上仍有习习凉风，难怪当地人称之为凉桥。走过凉桥仿佛穿越时光走廊，进入明清小镇。苔痕斑驳的古街上，千余间传统川南商肆民居檐牙相啄、错落有致，连绵起伏的小青瓦间露出一线天空。千年历史留给古镇龙华寺、禹王宫等众多古迹，其中最独特的，莫过于明末雕凿于八仙山崖壁之上的世界第一立佛。这尊深浮雕接引佛像高三十二米，体态丰盈、眉目安详，默立于丹山碧水间，聆听数百年间风吟溪唱。每年正月十四，龙华的妇女们会在大佛下起香，然后到凉桥上踩桥祈福。"女子踩桥"的民俗在龙华已经传承数百年，传递着人们对幸福的祈盼。

Longhua Ancient Town in Pingshan County was built in the Song Dynasty and took its present form during the Ming and Qing dynasties. It had been a major border town in Sichuan in many eras. The ancient town has mountains on one side and waters on the other. The Dalongxi and Xiaolongxi (the Big and Little Dragon Streams), which originate from Laojun (Supreme Lord Lao) Mountain, converge here. The Jinghong (Peaceful Rainbow) Bridge, which has been lying on the stream for over one hundred years, is antique, elegant, and beautiful, with ancient towering banyans on both banks. It is no wonder that the local people name it the Liangqiao (Cool) Bridge as there is still a cool breeze on the bridge on scorching summer days. Walking across the Liangqiao Bridge is like walking through a corridor of time into a town of the Ming and Qing dynasties. On the moss-streaked ancient street, more than one thousand traditional southern Sichuan shops and residential buildings see their projecting tiles connected in attractive disorder. A line of the sky is revealed between the small and undulating green tiles. Its millennium-old history has bestowed the ancient town with the Longhua (Dragon Resplendence) Temple, King Yu (Yu the Great) Palace, and many other monuments. Among others, the most unique one is the world's first standing Buddha, carved into the cliff of Baxian (Eight Immortals) Mountain in the late Ming Dynasty. This deep-relief Buddha statue is thirty-two meters high, with a plump body and a serene countenance, standing silently among the red mountains and the blue waters and listening to the chanting wind and streams over centuries. On the 14th day of the first month of every year, the women in the Longhua Temple will start burning joss sticks under the large Buddha statue and then go to tread the Cool Bridge to pray for blessings. The folklore of "women stepping on the bridge" has been passed down for centuries in Longhua, conveying people's prayers for happiness.

重庆
Chongqing

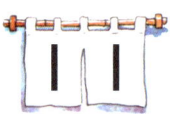

龚滩：乌江画廊，绝壁古镇
Gongtan: Gallery-like Land along the Wujiang River, with Exceptional Walls of an Ancient Town

20 世纪 80 年代，国画大师吴冠中顺着乌江一路写生，发现在东岸绝壁之上竟有一个风光绝世的千年古镇，并由此创作了《乌江小镇》《老街》等画作，将龚滩古镇永远定格在了画布之上。重庆酉阳龚滩古镇源起于蜀汉，明清时期因靠急流险滩成为乌江流域的货物转运站，商贾云集日益繁盛，来往客商也将汉文化带到了这个土家族苗族聚居地。数百年繁华给龚滩留下了众多名胜古迹，深藏峡谷的位置使古镇保留了目前中国最大的干栏式建筑群。走入古镇，只见依附陡峭山势而建的土家吊脚楼高低错落，河岸上赤褐色的干栏密布如林。盘横交错的老街随山形蜿蜒曲折，西秦会馆、董家祠堂、夏家院子和川主庙等明清建筑静立于岁月的尘雾中，隐藏起昔日的无限荣光。

In the 1980s, Wu Guanzhong (1919–2010), a traditional Chinese painting master, was sketching along the Wujiang River and discovered a millennium-old town on the cliff of the eastern bank. It inspired him to create paintings such as *A Small Town of Wujiang River* and *The Old Street*. These paintings set the Gongtan Ancient Town on canvas forever. Located in Youyang, Chongqin, Gongtan Ancient Town was originated in the Shu Han period (c. 221–263) of the Three Kingdoms. In the Ming and Qing dynasties, it became a transit for goods in the Wujiang River basin, where merchants gathered, flourished, and brought Han culture to this settlement of the Tujia and Miao ethnic groups. The prosperity lasting for centuries has left Gongtan with many famous monuments. Its location deep in the gorge has allowed the ancient town to retain the largest group of *Ganlan* (supported by pillars) buildings in China at present. As you stroll into the town, you will see the pillar-supported buildings of the Tujia ethnic group built on the steep mountain features, with a multitude of reddish-brown pillars on the river banks. The crisscrossing ancient streets twist and turn with the mountain features. The buildings of the Ming and Qing dynasties, such as the Xiqin Guildhall, the Dong Family Ancestral Hall, the Xia Family Courtyard and the Temple of the Chuanzhu (Protecting God of Sichuan) stand quietly in the dusty mist of the years, hiding the infinite glory of the past.

龙潭：民族风情，人杰地灵
Longtan: Ethnic Conditions and Customs on Remarkable Land with Outstanding People

　　酉阳龙潭古镇坐落于武陵山腹地中，因伏龙山下有两个状如"龙眼"的氽水洞积水成潭，古镇自龙眼之间穿过，形如龙鼻，因而得名。古镇始建于蜀汉，是土家族、苗族聚居地，清代发展为商业重镇，时人谓"龙潭货、龚滩钱"。抗战时期国民政府多个机构迁址于此，车马如龙的龙潭一时有"小南京"之称。历史风云变幻，岁月带走了繁荣商机，却留下了古老建筑。龙潭是目前重庆保存最完好、规模最大的古镇。走在龙潭光滑如镜的石板老街上，古老的海生物化石隐约可见。一百五十余堵层层叠叠的封火墙把古镇隔成了两百多个古朴清雅的四合院，赵世炎故居、王剑虹故居和丁玲笔下的酉阳中学皆在其中。五十余座飞檐翘角的土家吊脚楼零落散布其间，形成特有的多民族建筑风格。古镇民族风情浓郁，春节灯会火树银花，小端阳龙舟竞渡，大端阳跑旱龙船，展示了龙潭人多彩的民俗文化。

　　Located in Youyang, Longtan Ancient Town is in the hinterland of the Wuling Mountain. At the foot of Fulong (Crouching Dragon) Mountain, two ponds look like "dragon eyes". Passing like a dragon's nose through the two dragon eyes, the ancient town is given such a name. The ancient town was built in the Shu Han period (c. 221–263) of the Three Kingdoms. It is an inhabited land of the Tujia and Miao ethnic groups. It developed into a major commercial town in the Qing Dynasty with a widespread notion of "goods from Longtan and wealth in Gongtan". During the War of Resistance Against Japanese Aggression (1937–1945), the Nanjing-based National Government moved many of its agencies to this area, so that Longtan, with its endless traffic, was known as "Little Nanjing" for a while. With rapid changes in history, the years have taken away prosperous business opportunities but left behind ancient buildings. Longtan is currently the best-preserved and largest ancient town in Chongqing. Sauntering on the smooth, mirror-like stone streets of Longtan, you will find ancient fossilized sea creatures faintly visible. Over one hundred and fifty overlapping firewalls separate the ancient town into more than two hundred antique and elegant courtyards, including the Former Residence of Zhao Shiyan (1901–1927, a Chinese revolutionist), the Former Residence of Wang Jianhong (1901–1924, a Chinese social activist), and the Youyang High School in the literary work of Ding Ling (1904–1986, a Chinese novelist). More than fifty pillar-supported buildings with overhanging eaves and cornices built by the Tujia ethnic group are scattered throughout the area, forming a unique multi-ethnic architectural style. The ancient town features a strong ethnic flavor, with displays of fireworks and lanterns on the Spring Festival and the Lantern Festival; the dragon boat race on the Small Dragon Boat Festival (the fifth day of the fifth month); and the land dragon boat race at the Big Dragon Boat Festival, showcasing the colorful folk culture of the people of Longtan.

13 中山：山居菁华，桫椤王国

Zhongshan: Essence of Living in a Mountain and Kingdom of Cyathea

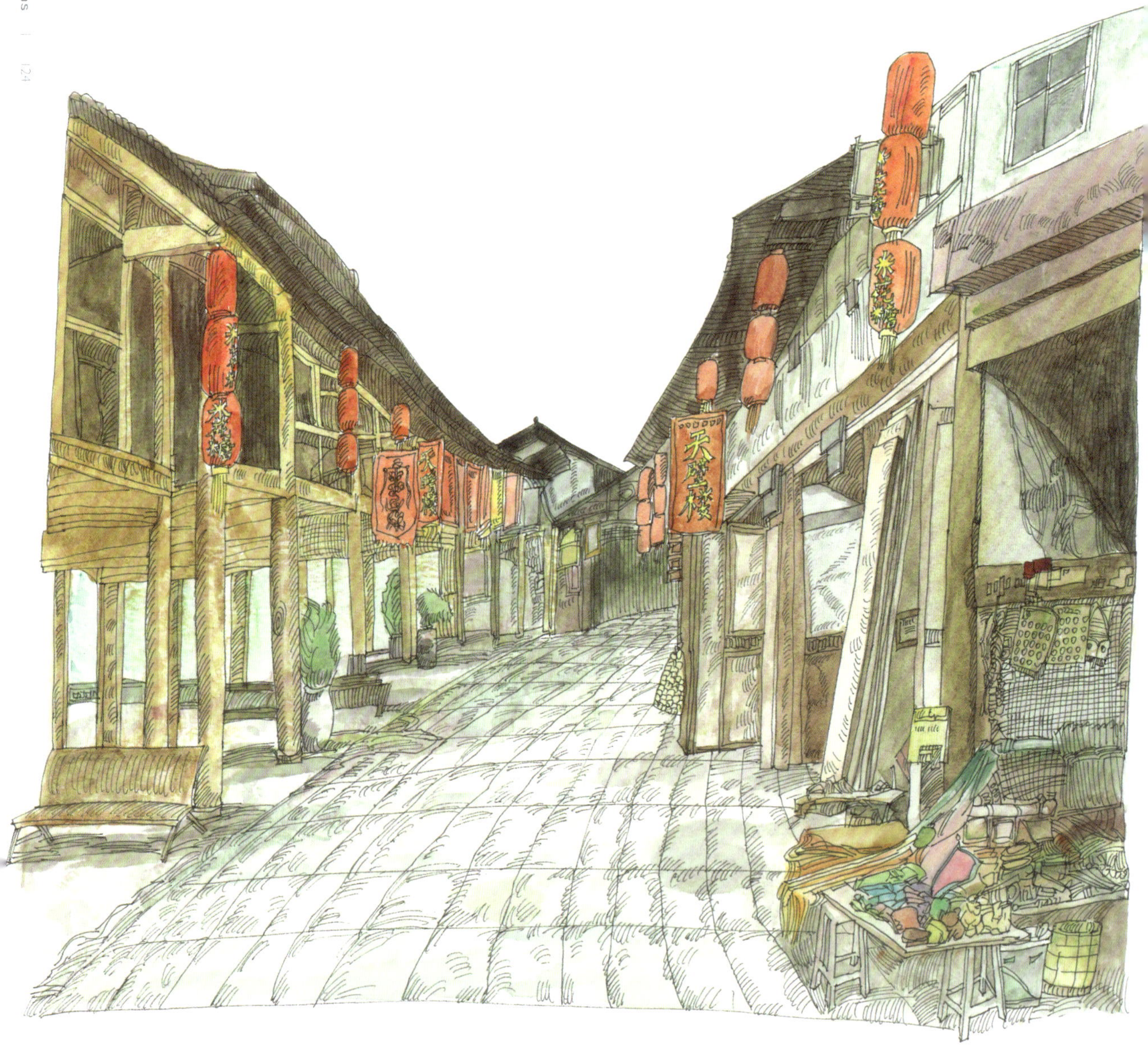

中山古镇位于川、渝、黔交界处的笋溪河畔,与国家级风景名胜区四面山一脉相连。古镇历史悠久,早在新石器时代即有先民在此劳动生息。中山俗称三合场,因水陆两便,自古是商贸兴旺的水陆码头,作为川黔山区的商品集散地,曾享千年繁华。往日的车船喧嚣早已成为历史,如今这座藏于深山的小镇保留着最古朴真淳的风貌,这里有西南地区规模最大、保存最完好、最具民族特色的山地民居古建群,庄园、古寨、古堡、寺庙、古桥星罗棋布。依河而建的老街青石为基,三百余间明清商铺民居红漆木板、竹篾夹墙,高低错落的吊脚楼巧妙地镶嵌于山水间,构成一幅风情浓郁的明清巴渝画卷。在距古镇二十余里的原始森林中,深藏着距今六千五百万年的侏罗纪大裂谷。林中两万多亩珍奇的桫椤树,如活化石般陪伴着古镇的千年兴衰。

Located on the shores of the Sunxi (Bamboo Shoot) Stream at the junction of Sichuan, Chongqing, and Guizhou, Zhongshan Ancient Town is adjacent to Simian (Four Sides) Mountain, a national scenic area. The ancient town features a long history, with ancestral people living and working here as early as the Neolithic era. Zhongshan, commonly known as Sanhechang, has been a thriving land and water terminal for trade and commerce since ancient times. It has enjoyed one thousand years of prosperity as a distribution center for goods from the mountainous areas of Sichuan and Guizhou. The hustling and bustling transport of the past has long since become history. At present, this small town, hidden in the mountains, has retained its most simple and unadorned features. It has the largest, best-preserved, and most ethnically featured ancient mountain residential buildings in the southwest of China. It is dotted with manors, ancient villages, ancient forts, temples, and ancient bridges. The ancient street built by the river has a foundation of green stones, with over 300 shops and residential buildings of the Ming and Qing dynasties whose walls are covered with red-painted wooden panels and woven bamboo strips. In attractive disorder, the pillar-supported buildings are cleverly set among the landscape, forming a richly flavored painting of Sichuan in the Ming and Qing dynasties. Deep in the primeval forest more than twenty li away from the ancient town, lies the Jurassic Rift Valley, which can be traced back to 65 million years old. More than 20,000 mu (around 1,333 hectares) of rare Cyathea trees in the forest, like living fossils, have accompanied the rises and falls of the ancient town for millennia.

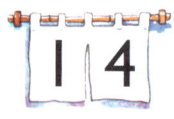

14 涞滩：蜀中二佛，瓮城巍峨
Laitan: Second Buddha in Sichuan with Towering 'Urn City'

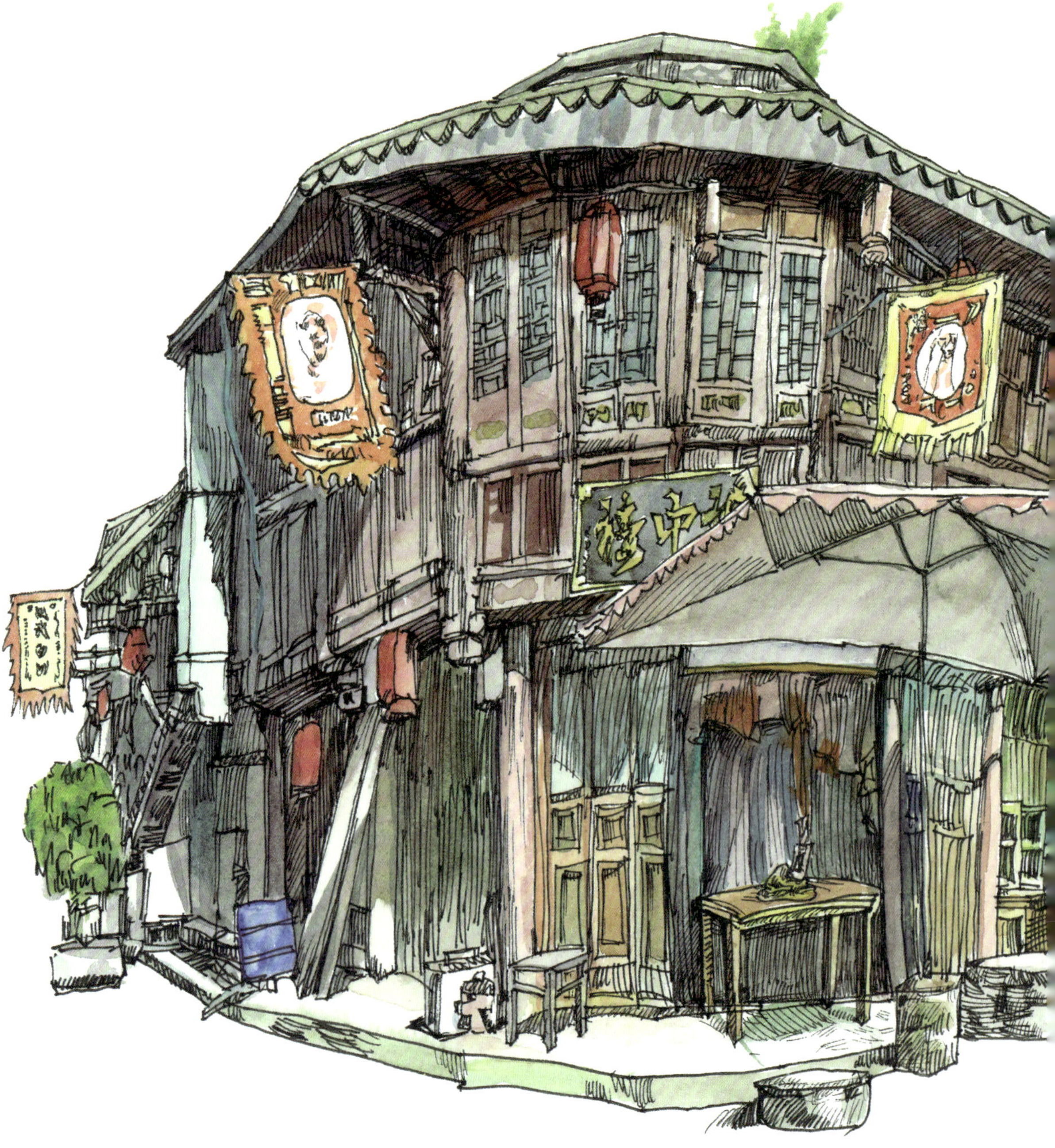

重庆涞滩古寨位于渠江之畔，建镇于宋代，现存规模形成于清咸丰年间。古寨有上、下涞滩之分，其间相隔咫尺。下涞滩紧靠渠江码头，百年前舟楫如云、街市繁华，现仍有四百余间清代民居静立于古朴老街。上涞滩位于鹫峰山顶，建造者利用三面峭壁的地势以石垒寨，构成坚固的防匪御敌工事。同治年间增修之时又建双道围城，深具兵法智慧，对敌有"瓮中捉鳖"之效，故名瓮城。瓮城是目前巴渝地区唯一保存完好的古代军事防御工事。涞滩古迹众多，其中以千年古刹二佛寺最闻名遐迩。寺中依岩镌凿的释迦牟尼金身高十余米，仅次于乐山大佛，被称为"蜀中第二佛"。二佛寺曾是四川最大的禅宗道场，也是我国规模最大的佛教禅宗造像聚点。寺中四十二龛窟一千七百余尊南宋石刻造像细腻传神、眉目如生，是我国第三石刻艺术高潮的代表作，堪称世间绝响。

Located on the banks of the Qujiang River, Chongqing, Laitan Ancient Village was built as a town in the Song Dynasty, with the existing scale formed during Emperor Xianfeng's reign (1850–1861) in the Qing Dynasty. The ancient village is divided into Shanlaitan and Xialaitan, which are separated by a stone's throw. Xialaitan is right next to the Qujiang River Dock. As a bustling market frequented by a multitude of cargo ships one hundred years ago, it still has over 400 residential buildings of the Qing Dynasty standing quietly on the antiquely simplistic old street. Shanglaitan is located at the top of the Jiufeng (Vulture Peak) Mountain, where the builders used stones to construct a stronghold with three cliff sides, turning it into a strong defense against bandits and other enemies. During Emperor Tongzhi's reign (r. 1861–1875), it was expanded with two walls. Being known for its wisdom in the art of war, it is named the "urn city" for its effect like "catching a turtle in an urn" against enemies. The Urn City is currently the only well-preserved ancient military stronghold in Sichuan. Laitan has been famous for its assorted monuments, including the Erfo (Second Buddha) Temple with a history of over one thousand years. In the temple, the golden body of Sakyamuni engraved in the rocks is more than ten meters high, second only to the Giant Stone Buddha at Leshan Mountain in Sichuan Province. It has been known as the "Second Buddha of Sichuan". The Erfo Temple was once the largest Zen Buddhist site for Buddhist rites in Sichuan and the largest gathering place of Zen Buddhist statues in China. In the temple, over 1,700 stone statues in forty-two niche caves of the Southern Song Dynasty are exquisite and vivid. As representatives of the third-wave culmination of the stone carving art in China, they deserve to be hailed as masterpieces of the world.

15 万灵：巴渝古寨，移民水乡
Wanling: Ancient Village in Sichuan and Waterside Town of Migrants

万灵古镇原名路孔镇，隶属重庆荣昌区。古镇青山环抱碧水萦回，濑溪河斜贯全境，北宋时期便是商贾云集的水码头。清代在此修筑了大荣寨，城墙四面设寨门，其中狮子门和日月门存留至今。明清老街在水码头的基础上扩建而成，自山顶蜿蜒而下，直达濑溪河边。老街不长，古迹却很多。万灵是清代"湖广填四川"的集散地，移民文化博大精深。功能丰富的湖广会馆曾收藏了多少移民的人生百味，弘阔精美的赵氏宗祠见证着皇族后裔的移民传奇。穿过"一线天"式的烟雨巷，携一身诗意踏出日月门，眼前便是平静开阔的濑溪河，河上是著名的大荣桥。古桥造型独具匠心，中间拱桥，便于行船；两边平桥，利于行人。青石板那一道道深深的踏痕，是大荣桥数百年的风霜印记。冬季水上浓雾弥漫，遥望桥上路人如悬空而行，是古镇奇妙一景。

Wanling Ancient Town, formerly known as Lukong Town, is under the jurisdiction of Rongchang District, Chongqing. The ancient town is surrounded by green hills and blue water, with the Laixi River flowing diagonally through the entire territory. During the Northern Song Dynasty, it was a waterside dock gathering merchants in large crowds. During the Qing Dynasty, the Darong Village was built here, with gates on four sides of the town walls, of which the Shizi (Lion) Gate and the Riyue (Sun and Moon) Gate have survived to this day. The waterside dock was expanded with the ancient streets of the Ming and Qing dynasties which wind down from the top of the hill to the banks of the Laixi River. The ancient street is not long, but there are many monuments. Wanling was the distribution center of "filling Sichuan with the people from Huguang (Hunan, Hubei, Guangdong, and Guangxi)", with a rich and profound immigrant culture. The richly functional Huguang Guildhall housed the assorted life experiences of many immigrants, while the spacious and exquisite Zhao Clan Ancestral Hall bore witness to the legends of immigrants of imperial descent. After sauntering through the Yanyu (Mist and Rain) Alley like "one thin strip of the sky", you will step out of the Sun and Moon Gate with a poetic feeling and see the calm and open Laixi River right before you, over which is the famous Darong Bridge. The ancient bridge is uniquely shaped, with an arch in the middle to facilitate boat traffic and a flat bridge section on either side to facilitate pedestrian traffic. The deep tread marks on the green stone slabs are the marks of centuries of natural elements endured by the Darong Bridge. In winter, when the water is permeated with thick mist, you will have a wonderful sight of the ancient town where the people are walking on the bridge as if they are suspended in the air.

16 西沱：千里盐道，云梯登天
Xituo: Thousand-Mile Salt Road with Scaling Ladder Reaching Heaven

重庆石柱县西沱古镇原名西界沱，古为"巴州之西界"，因地临长江南岸回水沱而得名。西沱自古是长江上游的深水良港，汉代已建码头；宋代成为千里盐道的起点，是自贡井盐的转运经销站，时人谓之"盐镇"；明清时期发展为"水陆贸易，烟火繁盛"的商贸重镇。往日繁华已随江风而逝，那些古老的商号、民居、会馆、寺观、衙署……如今成了游客眼中凝固的历史、流动的风景。西沱是长江沿线唯一的云梯式场镇，主街从江边垂直向上，攀缘五里达平坦地势，从街脚仰望如一挂云梯直插苍穹，因此得名"云梯街"，也被称为"万里长江第一街"。沿街拾级而上，仿佛从凡尘走入云端，两旁飞檐翘角的明清土家吊脚楼层层叠叠，雕梁画栋的庙堂会馆隐约可见，恍若天宫仙境。

Under the jurisdiction of Shizhu County of Chongqing, Xituo Ancient Town was formerly known as Xijietuo. Called the "western boundary of Bazhou Prefecture (Sichuan)," it was named after its location in the Huishuituo (Water-Returning Rock) on the southern bank of the Yangtze River. Xituo has been a deep-water port in the upper reaches of the Yangtze River since ancient times, with a wharf built in the Han Dynasty. It became the starting point of the Thousand-Mile Salt Road in the Song Dynasty. Being the transit and distribution station for Zigong's well salt, it was then called the "Salt Town". It developed into a major trade town in the Ming and Qing dynasties, with "thriving water and land trade amid its prosperous living scenes". The prosperity of the past has faded with the river breeze. Those antique shops and stores, residential buildings, guildhalls, temples, and government offices... have now become a solidified history and an undulating landscape in the eyes of tourists. Xituo is the only scaling ladder-style trading town along the Yangtze River. Its main street goes up vertically from the river, climbing five li to the flat terrain. Looking up from the foot of the street, you will see that it looks like a scaling ladder straight leading into the sky, hence the name of "the Scaling Ladder Street". Besides, it has also been hailed as "the first street on the ten-thousand-mile-long Yangtze River". Walking up the street, you seem to be walking from the earth into the clouds. On both sides are pillar-supported buildings with their overhanging eaves and cornices. They were built by the Tujia ethnic group in the Ming and Qing dynasties. The richly ornamented temples and guildhalls are faintly visible, making it look like a heavenly palace.

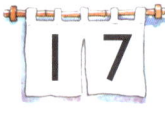

17 双江：双溪绕城，忠烈遗风

Shuangjiang: Twin Streams Around the City with Legacy of Loyalty and Martyrdom

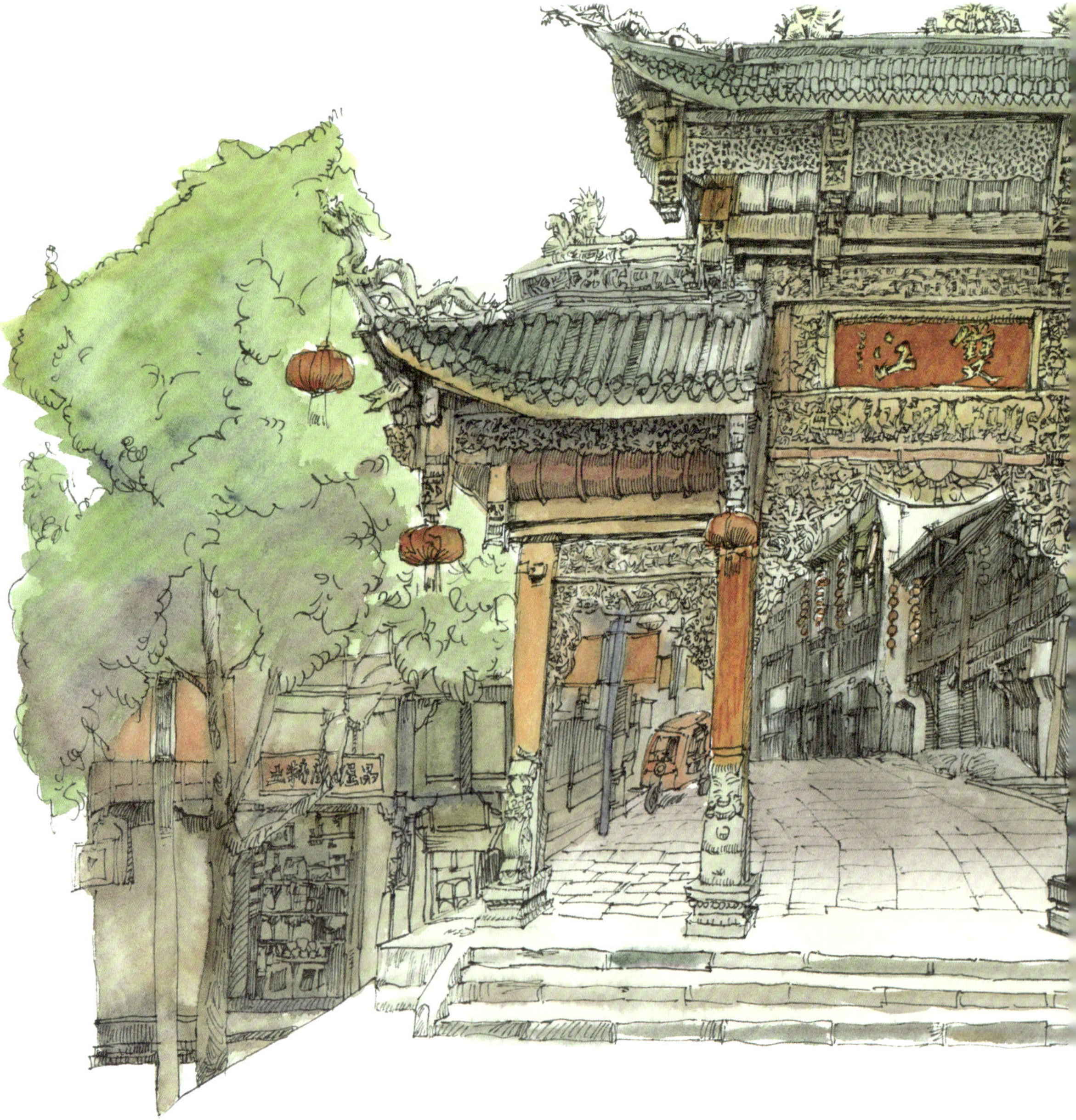

　　渝西北双江古镇建于明末清初，前临涪江、运河，镇内有猴溪、浮溪，因此得名"双江"。因舟楫便利风景清幽，清代民国多有富贵人家于此筑园置业，古镇上富丽精致的深宅大院星罗棋布，庭院深深隐于高墙之下。建于晚清的兴隆街大院如今已辟为民宿，来此可体验旧式的风雅生活。步入院中处处可入画，重重四合院落开阔轩朗，天井花木葱茏，屋宇雕饰精美，家具华贵雅致，令人流连忘返。除了二十余座清代大宅，这里还有蒋介石的行辕、白崇禧的官邸，都是当年国民政府内迁重庆时留下的。双江最值得驻足的是革命烈士杨闇公的旧居陈列馆。杨闇公是中共第一届四川省委书记，1926年领导了顺泸起义，次年慷慨就义时才二十九岁，他的铮铮铁骨和爱国精神永远激励着后来者。

　　Built in the late Ming and early Qing dynasties, Shuangjiang Ancient Town is located in northwest Chongqing, with Fujiang River and Yunhe River before it and Houxi Stream and Fuxi Stream inside it, hence the name "Shuangjiang". Due to the convenience of its water transport, many rich and noble families built gardens and procured properties here in the Qing Dynasty and the Republic of China period. The ancient town is dotted with fabulous and exquisite mansions, with courtyards hidden deep behind high walls. Built in the late Qing Dynasty, the compound on Xinglong Street has now been turned into guesthouses, where you can experience the old-fashioned elegance of life. After entering the courtyard, you will find it picturesque everywhere with its spacious, bright, and airy quadrangle courtyard, lush patio, beautifully decorated buildings, and luxurious and elegant furniture, where you might linger on with no intent to leave. In addition to over twenty mansions from the Qing Dynasty, there is also Chiang Kai-shek's (1887–1975, a military leader, head of the Nationalist government in China) field headquarters and Bai Chongxi's (1893–1966, a leader of Guangxi warlord faction, top Nationalist general) official residence, all of which were left behind when the National Government moved to inner parts of Chongqing. The worthiest destination in Shuangjiang is the Exhibition Hall of the Former Residence of Revolutionary Martyr Yang An'gong (1898–1927). Yang An'gong was the Secretary of the First Sichuan Provincial Committee of the Communist Party of China. He led the Luzhou-Shunqing Uprising in 1926. He was only 29 years old when he graciously gave his life the following year, with his unyielding spirit and patriotism always inspiring the future generations.

第五章
Chapter 5

湘黔胜景
Wonderful Scenery of Hunan and Guizhou

湖南
Hunan

凤凰古城：田园牧歌，最美小城
Fenghuang Ancient Town: Most Beautiful Town with Pastoral Scenes

　　若想探寻沈从文笔下的世外桃源，莫如去他的家乡湘西凤凰古城。这座"中国最美丽的小城"始建于明朝，虽历经四百余年沧桑但容颜依旧，是中国西南文物建筑最多的县份，也是土家族苗族聚居之地。从古城北门渡头登上乌篷船，沿沱江顺流而下，江水碧如寒玉，远眺西南群山，似有凤凰振翅欲飞，古城正由此得名。两岸悬于江上百余年的木质吊脚楼高低错落，黄永玉依古法建造的画室夺翠楼飞檐峭山，与明清吊脚楼浑然一体、古韵悠长。船行至古城的中心，便是气势恢宏的百年石拱桥——虹桥，桥上风雨楼一层为长廊，登临二层便可饱览风景，亦可欣赏楼中的名家收藏，山水与诗画于此交相辉映。听罢甜脆的苗歌对唱，船已荡过回龙潭，至望江亭登岸，踏上青石铺就的石板老街，访一访熊希龄故居和田家祠堂，拜谒一下沈从文的故居和墓地，感受在灵秀山川间人文蔚起的清雅气象。

If you want to explore the paradise that Shen Congwen (1902–1988, a Chinese novelist) wrote about, there is no better way than to visit his hometown, the Fenghuang Ancient Town in western Hunan. Built in the Ming Dynasty, this "most beautiful town in China" has survived the vicissitudes of over 400 years. It is the county with the largest number of cultural heritage buildings in southwest China and is home to the Tujia and Miao ethnic groups. From the ferry station at the north gate of the ancient town, you can board a dark-awninged boat and follow the Tuojiang River downstream. Along the journey, you will see the river as blue as cold jade and the mountains in the southwest looking like phoenixes fluttering their wings to take off. This is why the ancient town was known as Fenghuang (Phoenix) Ancient Town. On both sides of the river are wooden pillar-supported buildings that have been there in attractive disorder for more than one hundred years. Duocui (Green-Grasping) Building, the painting room built by Huang Yongyu (born in 1924, a Chinese artist) in accordance with ancient methods, shows its overhanging eaves and steep gables, which blends well together with the pillar-supported buildings of the Ming and Qing dynasties to produce a lingering appeal. When the boat reached the center of the ancient town, you will see the Hongqiao (Rainbow) Bridge, a magnificent century-old stone arch bridge. On the bridge is the Fengyu (Wind and Rain) Building, whose first floor is a promenade. On the second floor, you can admire the scenery and appreciate the collections of famous artists in the building, where the landscape, poetry, and pictorial art meet and add radiance and beauty to each other. After listening to the sweet and melodious songs of the Miao ethnic group sing in antiphonal style, you will see the boat passing the Huilong (Dragon-Returning) Pond. You can disembark at the Wangjiang (River-Gazing) Pavilion, where you can step onto the ancient street paved with bluestones, visit the Former Residence of Xiong Xiling (1870–1937, a Chinese politician) and the Ancestral Hall of the Tian Clan, and pay a visit to the Former Residence and Grave of Shen Congwen to experience the fresh and elegant atmosphere of humanities amid the delicately beautiful mountains and rivers.

02 芙蓉镇：王者之地，银河落天
Furong Town: Land of Kings with Waterfalls Like the Milky Way Falling from Heaven

在湘西永顺县酉水之阳，有一片飞檐翘角的古雅吊脚楼群，挂在声势如雷的飞瀑悬崖之上，美如天上宫阙，这里就是土司王朝旧都所在——王村。王村自古是"楚蜀通津"，有两千三百年历史。近代水运式微后，谢晋导演的《芙蓉镇》使这个沉寂多时的古镇名扬四海，地名也改为芙蓉镇。穿镇而过的是湘西最大的瀑布，急流直下如坠雪千堆，晴空下飞虹相映、七彩纷呈。从瀑布后面的栈道走过，水帘遇乱石嶙峋如万斛珍珠从天撒落，亦奇亦美别有洞天。随雪瀑蜿蜒而上，便可至峭壁之上的土司王行宫。土家楼群檐角高翘于奇山秀水间，寂寥中隐隐有龙虎之气，似在诉说主人昔日的辉煌。土司王是中国历史上存在时间最长的少数民族王朝。镌刻土司战争史的溪洲铜柱历经千年风侵水浸，铭文仍历历可见，是土家人的神物。走在古老的青石板街上，尝一碗酸辣的米豆腐，仿佛走进了电影场景中，亦真亦幻。

To the north side of Youshui River in Yongshun County, western Hunan, there is a cluster of elegant pillar-supported buildings with overhanging eaves and cornices. They are hanging from the cliffs with a thundering waterfall. Looking as beautiful as a heavenly palace, it is Wangcun Village, the old capital of the Tusi regime. Having been a "passageway between Hubei and Sichuan" since ancient times, Wangcun Village features a history of 2,300 years. After the decline of water transport in modern times, the film *Furong Town* directed by Xie Jin (1923–2008) made this long-dormant town famous, with its name changed to Furong Town. In the town is the largest waterfall in western Hunan, which flows straight down like a thousand heaps of falling snow. On a sunny day, there might be a colorful rainbow complementing the waterfall. Strolling through the path behind the waterfall, you will see that the water curtain meets the jagged rocks, causing the waterdrops to fall like a million pearls from the sky. It is a wonderful, beautiful, and rare sight. Following the snow-white waterfall to wind your way up the cliff, you will reach the Tusi King's Palace. The overhanging eaves of the buildings of the Tujia ethnic group are high up in the beautiful mountains and the water. In silence, they seem to reveal a majestic demeanor like that of a dragon and a tiger, as if telling about the past glory of their owners. The regime of the Tusi kings was the longest-standing minority one in Chinese history. The bronze pillars of Xizhou, engraved with the history of the Tusi wars, have survived thousands of years of natural elements, but the inscriptions are still visible. They are sacred to the people of the Tujia ethnic group. Sauntering along the ancient stone streets, you may also taste a bowl of spicy and sour rice tofu. It seems as if you have stepped into a movie scene to have a surreal experience.

德夯苗寨：苗疆明珠，飞瀑流纱
Dehang Miao Village: Pearl in the Miao Ethnic Group's Territory with Cascading Waterfalls like Flowing Silk Yarn

德夯苗寨隐于距湘西吉首四十余里的武陵山脉中，"德夯"在苗语中意为"美丽的峡谷"，这里山势跌宕、绝壁深壑、溪河交错、群峰叠嶂，有"小张家界"之名。在如斯美景中，苗寨依山而建，四面山势雄奇，九龙溪穿寨而过，跨过溪上古朴精巧的接龙桥，穿过一片灰瓦雕栏的苗家吊脚楼，可登壁立千仞的盘古峰。站于峰顶，无限风光尽收眼底。这里有车行云间的路桥奇观，有中国最高的流纱瀑布。飞瀑落差高达二百一十六米，水幕被山风吹得左右飘舞云蒸霞蔚，"流纱"二字言尽其妙。比山水更醉人的，是德夯浓郁的苗族风情。这里生活着八十多户苗家原住民，"接龙""斗牛""歌舞会"种种民俗异彩纷呈，最令人叫绝的还是苗族跳鼓。苗鼓是苗家供奉的圣物，是部落象征。忽急忽柔的鼓点，配以"脚跳手击腰旋体转"的豪放舞姿，将苗家人的生活劳作和喜怒哀乐，都融在了鼓中。

Dehang Miao Village is looming in the Wuling Mountain Ranges forty li away from Jishou, western Hunan. With "Dehang" referring to "a beautiful valley" in the Miao's language, this palace features uninhibited mountain landscapes, precipices with deep ravines, crisscrossing streams and rivers, and overlapping peaks, earning itself the reputation of being a "Small Zhangjiajie". Amid such a beautiful landscape, the Miao village was built against the imposing and uniquely featured mountains. With the Jiulong (Nine Dragons) Stream flowing through the village, you can cross over the antique and exquisite Jielong (Dragon-Greeting) Bridge. After passing a stretch of pillar-supported buildings with grey tiles and carved balustrades of the Miao ethnic group, you can ascend the Pangu Peak which rises steeply into thousands of feet. Standing atop the peak, you will have a panoramic view of the infinite scenery. Here, you can admire the marvelous spectacle of roads and bridges with vehicles shuttling amid clouds and the silk yarn-like waterfall with the greatest height in China. With a drop of over 216 meters, you can see the water curtain flying up in a magnificent landscape as it is wind-blown, fully revealing the wonder of the descriptions with the words of "the silk yarns". More intoxicating than the landscape is the rich flavor of the local conditions and customs of the Miao ethnic group in Dehang. Dwelled by over eighty aborigine households of the Miao ethnic group, this land sees a brilliant and varied display with various popular customs such as "greeting the dragon," "bullfights," and "song and dance parties". The most applauded one is the Jumping Drums of the Miao ethnic group. The Miao drums, which are the relics worshipped by the Miao ethnic group, are symbols of the tribes. Their features, such as the drumbeats alternating between urgency and softness and the bold and unrestrained dancing postures and movements from "jumping feet, striking hands, revolving waists, and circling bodies," have integrated various emotions of the people of the Miao ethnic group living and working here into the drumbeats.

04 里耶：秦简故里，湘西名镇
Liye: Hometown of the Bamboo Slips Used in the Qin Dynasty and a Famous Town in Western Hunan

湘西里耶古镇坐落于武陵山腹地酉水河畔。里耶，语出土家语，意为辟地；其附近的梅茶，意为开天，两者合为"开天辟地"。这里是土家族的发祥地，早在旧石器时代就有先民居住。清代形成了酉水流域有名的码头商埠，民国有"小南京"之誉。如今镇上的老街仍保留着明清建筑风貌，五百余幢土家民居古韵悠长。数百年繁华如过眼云烟，直到2002年在古井内出土了三万七千余枚秦简，里耶因此名动四海。这些秦简是以往出土秦简总数的十倍，内容涉及秦楚战争、经济民生、政治文化等方方面面，史料价值比肩于西安兵马俑。凭借这份详尽的洞庭郡迁陵县公文档案，人们终得一窥秦朝社会全貌。在里耶还发现了战国和两汉的古城遗迹、两汉的古墓群，小小一镇竟保存了数千年历史变迁留下的清晰印记，隐藏着楚湘文化的深厚底蕴。这是里耶独有的魅力，是岁月赠予的无价之宝。

In western Hunan, Liye Ancient Town is located on the bank of the Youshui River in the hinterland of the Wuling Mountain. Liye, with its origin in the language of the Tujia ethnic group, refers to opening up the Earth. Its nearby place named Meicha means opening up heaven. As a result, the combination of the two refers to "the creation of Heaven and Earth". As the place of origin for the Tujia ethnic group, it was already dwelled by the ancients as early as the Paleolithic Age. In the Qing Dynasty, it was formed as a wharf and a commercial port with a reputation in the Youshui River basin. During the Republic of China period, it was hailed as "Small Nanjing (then capital of the Republic of China)". At present, on the old streets of the town, buildings preserved the architectural features of the Ming and Qing dynasties, where over five hundred residential buildings of the Tujia ethnic group are characterized by their time-honored antique appeal. Centuries, as transient as a fleeting cloud, flitted. In 2002, over 37,000 bamboo slips of the Qin Dynasty were unearthed from ancient wells, earning global fame for Liye. These bamboo slips are ten times more than those of their kind unearthed in the past, involving so many aspects such as the warfare between the Qin kingdom and the Chu state, the economy and people's livelihood, politics, culture, among others that their value as historical materials is on an equal level with the Terracotta Army in Xi'an. This thorough and detailed official document of the Qinling County of the Dongting Prefecture offers glimpses into the full view of the society of the Qin Dynasty. Also discovered in Liye were ancient city sites from the Warring States period (475–221 BC) and the Han Dynasty and ancient tomb clusters of the Han Dynasty. Despite its small scale, this ancient town accommodates the preservations of clear marks displaying the historical changes over millennia and stores the profound deposits of the culture of Hubei and Hunan Provinces. Highlighting the unique charm of Liye, they are priceless treasures bestowed by time.

张谷英村：民间故宫，耕读继世
Zhangguying Village: Forbidden City in the Folk Passed on Generations by Farming and Reading

在湖南岳阳渭洞山区，隐藏着中国最独特的古村落。它以明洪武年间始迁祖张谷英命名，村中至今无一外姓，两千六百多名村民均系始祖后裔。古村四面青山环抱，渭溪河蜿蜒而过如"金带环抱"，构成完美的风水格局。村中现有明清建筑一千七百三十二间，屋宇雕梁画栋，合院纵横交织，各院之间有屏门檐廊和巷道沟通分隔，分则自成体系，合则为连体大宅。整个村落户户相通、远近分明，干枝式布局清晰体现了宗族血亲脉络，有"民间故宫"之誉。张氏家族历来崇文尚儒，村中当大门两侧的对联"耕读继世，孝友传家"，成为张氏后人世代相承的精神。村中人才辈出，读书人科甲联芳，入仕者无一贪官。张谷英村之珍贵，不仅在于它创造了中国民间建筑的奇迹，更在于它承载着中华传统文化之根，传递着"孝、和、勤、廉"的儒家精神。

In the Weidong mountainous area, Yueyang, Hunan Province, there hides the most distinct ancient village in China. Named after Zhang Guying, the first-generation ancestor of the village during the years of Emperor Hongwu, the village has been dwelled by over 2,600 descendants of Zhang, with no people of other surnames. Embraced by green mountains on all sides and "girdled by the golden belt" of the meandering Weixi River, the village features a perfect layout of Fengshui geomantic omen. In the villages, there are 1,732 preserved buildings of the Ming and Qing dynasties. The buildings are richly ornamented while the courtyards are crisscrossing, with screen doors, verandas, and alleys joining and separating them. In separation, each forms its own system; when joined, they become a one-piece mansion. Throughout the village, each household is connected, with distinct far and near views. The trunk-branch layout gives a clear reflection of the blood relations within the patriarch clan, earning itself the reputation of "the Forbidden City in the Folk". The Zhang Clan has been honoring culture, especially Confucianism. On both sides of the middle gate of the village are couplets that read "Continuing the generations with farming and reading; Sustaining families in filial piety and fraternity," which reflect the spirit passed on among the descendants of the Zhang Clan for generations. The village has witnessed talents coming forth in large numbers, with great achievements in the imperial civil examinations and with no corrupt officials among its descendants in the officialdom. Zhangguying Village is precious not only because it created the architectural miracles in China's folk society but also because it has carried the root of traditional Chinese culture, passing on the Confucian spirit of "filial piety, harmony, diligence, and incorruptibility".

贵州
Guizhou

06 镇远：山雄水美，龙舞端阳
Zhenyuan: Majestic Mountains and Beautiful Rivers with Dragon Dances on the Dragon Boat Festival

贵州镇远古镇坐落于武陵山崇山峻岭之中，碧绿的舞阳河呈S形穿城而过，形成独特的太极古城之貌。这座有两千三百多年历史的古镇地处入黔要道，自古既是商贸繁华的水陆都会，也是兵家必争的军事重镇。上千年来，客商使者南来北往，中原文化、边地民族文化、域外文化在此交融共生。这种融汇也体现在建筑上，镇远古民居是江南庭院和山地建筑的完美结合，"歪门邪道"最具风格。始建于明初的青龙洞依山而立、贴壁凌空，飞檐高翘于悬崖之上，雕窗面临幽幽碧水，荟萃天下山水楼阁，融儒释道三教为一体，是山地贴崖建筑的精华之作。镇远历史悠久、民俗丰富，端午节是镇远二十多个民族共同的节日，舞阳河上的龙舟赛从明代传承至今，已被列入国家非遗名录。每年端午，舞阳河上百舸争流、万民同乐，是难得一见的盛景。

Zhenyuan Ancient Town is located in the lofty ridges and towering mountains of Wuling Mountain, Guizhou Province. With the green Wuyang River flowing in an S shape through the town, it gave rise to the ancient town uniquely featured by the Taoist *Taiji* (Supreme Ultimate). With a history of over 2,300 years, this ancient city is situated on a strategic thoroughfare to enter Guizhou Province. It has been a land and water metropolis with prosperous trade and commerce and a strategic military town soldiers contended for. For over one thousand years, merchants and emissaries have been traveling north and south via this ancient town, thus enabling the cultural elements from the Central Plain, the ethnic groups from the borderlands, and the foreign regions to enjoy integration and symbiosis here. Such integration is also reflected in buildings. The ancient residential buildings of Zhenyuan see the perfect combination of the courtyards from the areas south of the Yangtze River and the buildings from mountainous regions. Their most usual characteristics are of the most distinct styles. The Qinglong (Green Dragon) Cave, built in the early years of the Ming Dynasty, stands beside mountains where it is high up in the sky on a precipice. Its upturned eaves overhang on the cliff, while its carved windows face the green river looming in the distance. As an epitome of the landscape buildings across China and an integration of the three doctrines including Taoism, Confucianism, and Buddhism, it is a masterpiece among buildings on precipices in mountainous areas. Zhenyuan features a time-honored history and rich folk customs. With the Dragon Boat Festival shared among over 20 ethnic groups in Zhenyuan, the Dragon Boat Race on the Wuyang River has been passed along from the Ming Dynasty and included in the national list of intangible cultural heritage. On the Dragon Boat Festival each year, the sight of hundreds of dragon boats contending amid the shared joy of the people is a rare grand view.

07 肇兴侗寨：鼓楼之乡，侗歌飞扬
Zhaoxing Dong Village: Hometown of Drum Towers with Reverberating Songs of the Dong Ethnic Group

　　黔东南肇兴侗寨四面青山环抱，梯田云雾缭绕，肇兴河穿寨而过，寨内碧水潆洄，鼓楼、花桥和杉木建造的侗族吊脚楼参差错落。早在八百多年前，即有先民生活在这方宝地。"未建寨，先建楼"，鼓楼是侗寨之魂，它如气势恢宏的宝塔矗立寨中，飞阁重檐、雕绘精绝，是侗族建筑艺术的瑰宝。肇兴鼓楼群在全国侗寨中绝无仅有。寨中五团建有五座各具风格的鼓楼，寨民们的人生大事几乎都在这里举办。侗族人能歌善舞，千百年来他们通过歌声来传承民族文化。已被列入世界非遗名录的侗族大歌，以十六声部无伴奏演唱为特点，模拟高山流水、虫鸣鸟叫、林海松涛、空谷回响等大自然之音，婉转起伏、广阔无穷，宛若天籁，被称为"清泉般闪光的音乐，掠过古梦边缘的旋律"。

　　Located in the southeast of Guizhou Province, Zhaoxing Dong Village is surrounded by green mountains on all sides, with terraced fields looming in cloud and mist. The Zhaoxing River flows through the village, adding it with crystal-clear and whirling water. The drum towers, richly ornamented bridges, and the pillar-supported fir wood buildings of the Dong ethnic group are in attractive disorder. The ancients began to live here as early as over eight hundred years ago. "The buildings were constructed before the formation of the village." As the soul of the Dong village, the drum towers stand like majestic pagodas. With their overhanging pavilions, double-eaved roofs, and exquisite and ingenious carved and painted elements, they are treasures of the architectural art of the Dong ethnic group. The Zhaoxing Drum Towers Cluster is the only one of its kind in all villages of the Dong ethnic group across China. At the five *Tuans* (sectors) of the village, five distinctly featured drum towers were built to serve as the venues for almost all major events of life for the villagers. The people of the Dong ethnic group excel in both singing and dancing, passing on their ethnic culture through singing for millennia. The Grand Song of the Dong ethnic group has been inscribed on the Representative List of the Intangible Cultural Heritage of Humanity. Featured by its 16-part singing without instrumental accompaniment, it imitates such natural sounds as high mountains and flowing water, cries of insects and birds, the soughing of the wind in the forests, echoes in empty valleys, among others. In its tactful rises and falls across an infinite range, it is just like producing the sounds of nature. It is hailed as "the music glittering like clear spring water and the melodies flitting across the edges of an ancient dream".

08 青岩：山地兵城，状元故里
Qingyan: Military Town in the Mountainous Areas and Hometown of Successful Candidates of the Imperial Civil Examinations at the highest level

贵阳青岩古镇坐落于贵州中部崇山峻岭间，始建于明洪武年间，因明朝屯兵而建镇，因附近多青色岩峰而得名，是一座因军事城防演化而来的山地兵城，素有贵阳"南大门"之称。

古镇依山就势，城墙用青条巨石筑于悬崖上，巍峨险要，跨越百年仍坚不可摧。从恢宏的广定门登上城墙，山水环抱中的古镇全貌尽收眼底。古镇民居多以石片当瓦、石块垒墙，目之所及一派青灰苍黑，难怪青岩有"石头城"之名。石头城硬朗的气质很适合拍战斗场面，电影《寻枪》就拍摄于此。青岩不仅是军事重镇，也是人文荟萃之地，贵州历史上第一个文状元赵以炯就出自这里。状元府气派而不张扬，大门上一副"琴鹤谱志，论语传家"的对联，彰显着书香门第的风范。青岩寺庙、道观极多，还有古老的天主教堂和基督教堂，多种宗教文化和谐共存，是中国古镇中极为罕见的风景。

Located amid the lofty ridges and towering mountains in Guiyang, central Guizhou Province, Qingyan Ancient Town was first built in the years of Emperor Hongwu of the Ming Dynasty. Built as a town for stationing troops in the Ming Dynasty, the Qingyan (Blue-green Rock) Ancient Town was named after abundant blue-green rock peaks in the neighboring areas. As a military town in the mountainous areas evolving with its purpose in military defense, it has been known as the "Southern Gate" of Guiyang.

The ancient town was built in line with the mountain features, with its town walls constructed with green boulders on cliffs. Towering in a strategic location, it is still indestructible after centuries. After ascending the town wall from the grand Guangding (Vast Firmness) Gate, you will have a panoramic view of the ancient town encircled by mountains and rivers. In the ancient town, the residential buildings have rock slabs as roof tiles and stones as walls. As one sees a stretch of dark and deep blue-green scenery, it is no wonder that Qingyan Ancient Town has been known as "the Stone Citadel". The robust temperament of the Stone Citadel makes it a perfect site for shooting battle scenes, with the movie titled *The Missing Gun* shot here. Qingyan is not only a place of military strategic importance but also a land with a gathering of talents, being the hometown of Zhao Yijiong (1857–1907), the first Number one scholar (candidate of the imperial civil examinations at the highest level) in the history of Guizhou. The mansion of Zhao is impressive but not flamboyant. On the gate is a pair of couplets that reads, "Zithers and cranes reveal the aspirations; Confucian classics pass on the family lineage," revealing the demeanor of this family of scholars. Qingyan Ancient Town, with abundant Buddhist and Taoist temples and antique Catholic and Protestant churches, sees the peaceful co-existence of multiple religious cultures, which is a rare sight among ancient towns in China.

09 岜沙：远古遗风，枪手部落
Basha: Customs Handed Down from the Remote Antiquity in a Tribe of Firearm Holders

　　黔东南从江县岜沙苗寨坐落于月亮山麓的林海之中，层层叠叠的吊脚楼掩映于苍翠山林间，五百余户人家至今延续着苗家远古遗风。寨头是一片古林，林中的百年古树是岜沙人生命的延续。"岜沙"在苗语中义为草木繁盛，岜沙人把树看作神灵，从不任意砍伐，离世后也采用树葬的方法回归自然。岜沙人皆身着自制的青布衣，女子穿亮光百褶裙扎绑腿，精美古雅的刺绣搭配娇艳镶边，灵动俏丽。岜沙汉子仍留着自蚩尤老祖时代传下的古老发髻，他们在成人礼上要用镰刀剃掉四周头发，仅留下中部盘发为鬏髻，从此保持一生。发髻象征着山上生长的树木，青布衣则象征着树皮。看到岜沙汉子肩扛火枪莫要吃惊，他们虽终身配枪但从不乱放，以前是为了狩猎，现在主要在庆典或迎宾时才会对天鸣枪。岜沙持枪是获得了公安机关特批的。

　　Basha Miao Village is located at the sea of trees at the foot of the Yueliang (Moon) Mountain, Congjiang County, southeastern Guizhou Province. Rows of pillar-supported buildings loom amid verdant mountain forests. Here, over five hundred households have preserved the customs handed down from the remote antiquity of the Miao ethnic group. Near the entrance of the village is a stretch of ancient forests, with the century-old ancient trees in the forests symbolizing the continuity of life of the people in Basha. In the language of the Miao ethnic group, the term "Basha" refers to verdant vegetation. Treating trees as deities and spirits, the people of Basha have never felled them arbitrarily. A person of Basha who passed away will go through a tree burial to return to Nature. Among the people of Basha dressed in self-made green cotton clothes, the women wear shining pleated skirts and leg wrappings with exquisite, classic, and elegant embroidery matched with delicate and charming rims, revealing their nimble and pretty demeanors. The men have their hair worn in a bun or coil, a practice passed down from the patriarch of Chiyou (legendary tribal leader during the time of Yellow Emperor reigning 2697–2597 BC). On their coming of age ceremonies, their side hair is shaved, leaving only the coiled hair in the middle as a bun which they wear throughout their life. While the buns symbolize the trees growing on mountains, the green cotton clothes are symbols of the tree bark. There is no need to be surprised by the sight of a man of Basha carrying a firearm. Despite the firearms, they have never fired a shot arbitrarily. While used to hunt, the firearms are fired to the sky during celebrations or reception of visitors. Their rights to hold firearms have been specially approved by the public security agency.

郎德上寨：英雄故里，苗歌嘹亮
Langdeshang Village: Hometown of Heroes with Resonant Songs of the Miao Ethnic Group

朗德上寨始建于明初，是全国第一个民俗风情村寨游览地，却并没有过度开发，仍保留着古朴天然的风貌。朗德隶属黔东南雷山县，青山环抱中，高低错落的苗家吊脚楼已矗立百年，清澈的巴拉河从寨前缓缓流过。苗家姑娘头饰银光闪闪，艳丽的百褶长裙上撒满精致绣花。盛装出迎的她们，在寨门前唱起了脆甜的敬酒歌，盛情之下游客难免要尝一尝那香醇的拦路酒了。入得寨中，可以欣赏到最丰富多彩的苗族歌舞。节奏明快的芦笙舞、粗犷灵活的铜鼓舞、俏丽多姿的锦鸡舞……游人常常情不自禁加入其中，陶醉在苗家歌舞的无穷魅力中。如今歌舞升平的朗德，当年曾是苗族英雄杨大六抗击清军的大本营。走进杨大六简朴的故居，抗清义士用过的刀枪剑戟就静静陈列在那里，仿佛在诉说百年前浴血奋战的悲壮历史。

Langdeshang Village, which was first built in the early years of the Ming Dynasty, is the first tourist ethnic-style village of folk conditions and customs in China. Without undergoing excessive commercial development, it still maintains its antiquely simplistic and natural features. Under the jurisdiction of Leishan County of southeastern Guizhou Province, Langde is surrounded by green mountains. Its pillar-supported buildings of the Miao Ethnic Group, which stand in attractive disorder, have been standing for centuries. The lucid Bala River flows gently before the village. Women of the Miao Ethnic Group wear glittering head ornaments and gorgeous pleated long skirts dotted with exquisite embroidery. In their splendid attires, they come out to greet the guest, singing the clear and sweet toasting songs before the stockade's gate. Facing their boundless hospitality, visitors cannot help tasting the rich and mellow waylaying wine. After entering the village, visitors can appreciate the richest and most colorful songs and dances of the Miao Ethnic Group featuring the lively rhythm bagpipes dances, the straightforward, uninhibited, and nimble bronze drum dances, and the beautiful and variably graceful pheasant dances... Visitors find it difficult to resist the temptation to join the dances and revel in the inexhaustible charm of the songs and dances of the Miao Ethnic Group. Langde, which enjoys peace and prosperity at present, served as the base camp of Yang Daliu (around 1855), a hero of the Miao Ethnic Group, to stage a peasant uprising against the Qing Dynasty. After entering the simple and unadorned former residence of Yang Daliu, you can see the weapons used by the high-minded persons against the Qing Dynasty such as swords, spears, arrows, and halberds quietly displayed there, as if telling the tragic and heroic history of fighting bloody battles centuries ago.

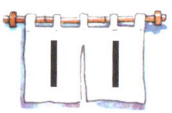

西江：千户苗寨，芦笙之乡
Xijiang: Miao Village with Over 1,000 Households and Hometown of the Reed-pipe Wind Instrument

　　西江苗寨静卧于苍莽的雷公山麓深处，有一千二百多户人家，是世界上最大的苗族聚居村寨。绿树掩映中，古朴的枫木吊脚楼从河边层层叠叠绵延至山顶，在重峦叠嶂间铺就气势恢宏的山地建筑奇观。清澈的白水河将苗寨一分为二，云雾缭绕间整座寨子如蝴蝶振翅欲飞。西江是芦笙之乡，清脆悠扬的芦笙，传递着小儿女的爱意，也传承着苗族千年文化。世代传唱的苗族古歌，如同一支包罗万象的苗族史诗。铸造银饰是西江汉子的传统绝活儿，通过掐丝、拉花等古法工艺手工打制的精美银饰，再配上精美的苗绣、淡雅的蜡染，把苗家姑娘衬得光彩夺目。酸汤鱼是苗家传统美食，点上一锅，看新鲜的鱼肉在沸腾的红酸汤内翻滚，香气扑鼻令人食指大动，吃上一口，酸辣麻香的滋味在舌尖跳跃。

　　Lying quietly in the depth of the foot of the vastly verdant Leigong (Thunder Deity) Mountain, the Xijiang Miao Village has over 1,200 households, being the largest village of the Miao ethnic group. Shaded by green trees, the antiquely simplistic pillar-supported buildings stretch in rows from the river bank to the mountaintop, thus presenting a majestic mountainous architectural spectacle amid range upon range of mountains. The lucid Baishui (White Water) River separates the whole village of the Miao ethnic group into two parts. Looming in the whirling clouds and mist, the whole village looks like a butterfly fluttering its wings to take off. Xijiang is hailed as the hometown of the reed-pipe wind instrument. The clear and melodious instrument sounds pass on the affections between people in love and inherit the millennium-old culture of the Miao ethnic group. The antique songs of the Miao ethnic group sung in numerous generations are like an all-inclusive epic of the ethnic group. It is a traditional unique skill of the men of Xijiang to cast silver ornaments. The exquisite silver ornaments manually made with filigree, garland, and other ancient techniques, coupled with delicate Miao embroidery and quietly elegant wax printing, add dazzling brightness to the women of the Miao ethnic group. Boiled Fish in Sour Soup is a traditional delicious dish of the Miao people. You may order a pot in which the fresh fish is boiled in the red sour soup, spreading such an intense fragrance around that your appetite will be fully aroused. With just one bite, you will feel a mixture of sour, hot, numbing, and fragrant tastes frolicking on your tongue.

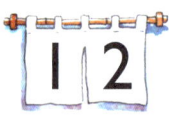

12 旧州：且兰古都，长征足迹
Jiuzhou: Ancient Capital of Qielan State, with Footprints of the Long March

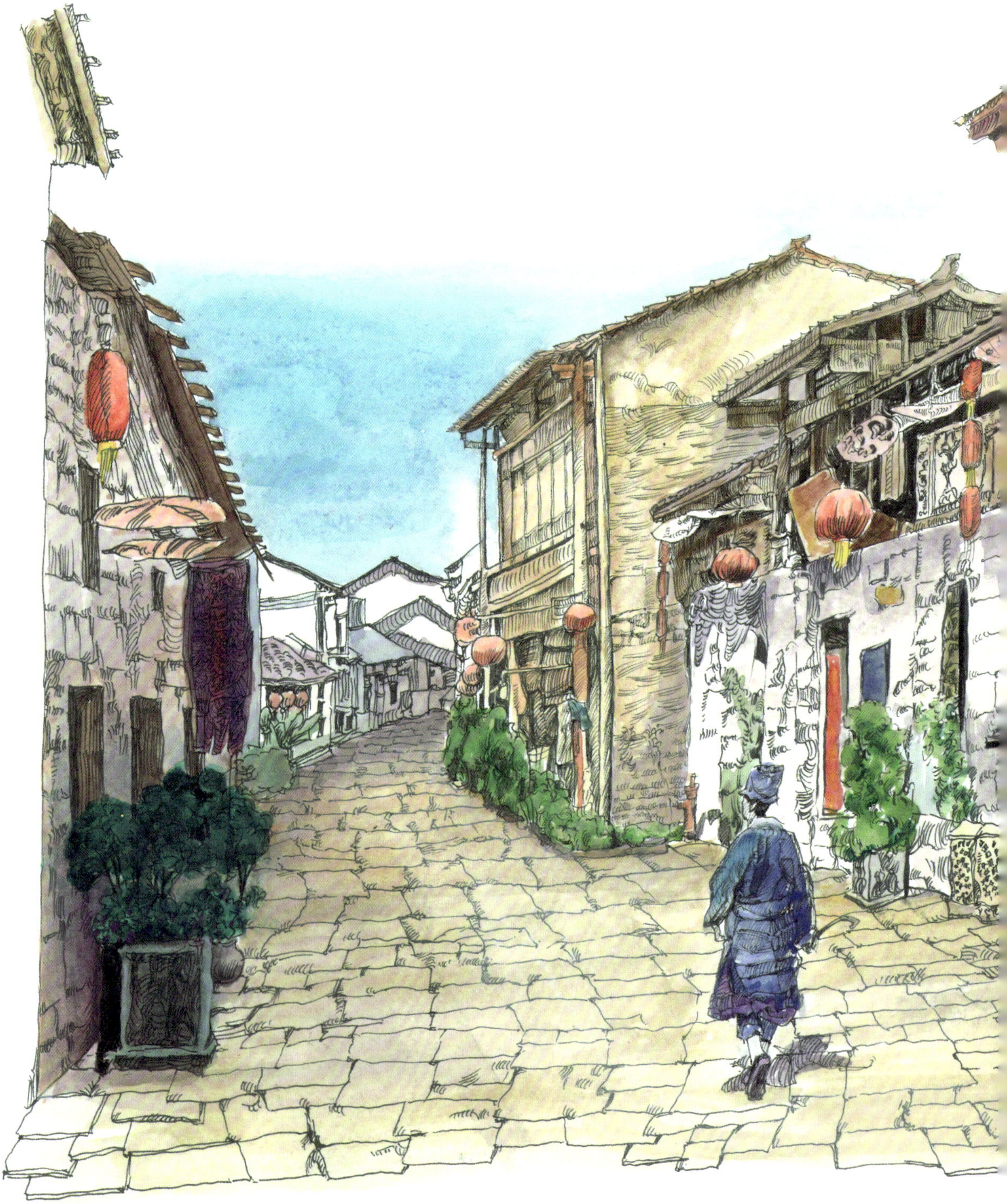

　　旧州古镇位于黔东南黄平县西北五十余里的舞阳河畔，距今已有两千三百多年历史，在周、春秋战国时为且兰国都城。明清时期旧州是黔东最繁华的通商码头，水陆交汇、商贾云集。商贸的繁荣促进了多种文化的融合，数百年的物阜民丰给旧州留下无数精美的庙宇会馆和民居商肆。今天古镇仍保留着许多明清建筑，残破和精致交织的老宅，华美恢宏的万寿宫，古朴典雅的文昌宫……仍默默吐露着昔日风华。颇为与众不同的是那座始建于乾隆年间的法式天主教堂。1934年，红六军团团长萧克在这里发现了一张法文版的贵州地图，地图十分详细，为红军顺利走出云贵发挥了重要作用。长征路上，毛泽东、周恩来、朱德等老一辈革命家都曾在这里留下足迹。

　　Jiuzhou Ancient Town is located on the bank of Wuyang River over fifty li away to the northwest of Huangping County, southeastern Guizhou Province. It has a history of over 2,300 years, being the capital of the Qielan State during the Zhou Dynasty (1046–256 BC), the Spring and Autumn period (770–476 BC) and the Warring States period (475–221 BC). During the Ming and Qing dynasties, Jiuzhou was the most prosperous wharf in eastern Guizhou, where the land and water transport intersect and merchants come together in crowds. The thriving business and trade have promoted the integration of multiple cultures. Centuries in which products abound and the people live in plenty have left numerous exquisite temples, guildhalls, residential buildings, and shops. At present, many buildings of the Ming and Qing dynasties have been well preserved in the ancient town, such as old residential buildings being broken and exquisite at the same time, the magnificent Wanshou (Longevity) Palace, and the antiquely simplistic and elegant Wenchang (Cultural Prosperity) Palace, and others which still reveal their past elegance and intellectual brilliance. An extraordinary building is the French-style Catholic Church built during the years of Emperor Qianlong. In 1934, Xiao Ke (1907–2008), commander of the No.6 Corps of the Red Army, discovered a Guizhou map in French. With its detailed records, the map played a significant role for the Red Army to march out of Yunnan and Guizhou. On the Long March, veteran revolutionists such as Mao Zedong (1893–1976, Chinese communist leader and founder of the PRC), Zhou Enlai (1898–1976, Chinese Communist leader, premier of the State Council from 1949 to 1976) and Zhu De (1886–1976, Chinese Communist leader and founder of the People's Liberation Army) left their footprints here.

第六章
Chapter 6

北方古韵
Antique Appeal of Northern China

山西
Shanxi

平遥古城：华夏文明，晋商遗韵
Pingyao Ancient City: Land of Chinese Civilization with the Lasting Appeal of the Shanxi Merchants

晋中平遥古城古称陶，相传是尧帝的初封之地。始建于西周，现存明清建筑近四千座，作为中国保存最为完整的古城，堪称华夏文明的典型代表。登上明洪武年间修筑的古老城墙，眼前一幅鲜活的明清县城长卷徐徐展开。长街曲巷密如棋盘，精致宏阔的深宅大院错落其间。位于中轴线上的南大街，是19世纪末中国的华尔街。票号、钱庄、当铺、布店、药堂……南大街上几乎包罗了明清所有商业行当。明末晋商的生意已遍及天下，平遥富商巨贾云集。1823年，中国第一家票号"日升昌"在平遥应运而生，随后票号越来越多，平遥成了中国当时的金融中心。1997年与古城一并加入世界文化遗产的，还有城外两座千年古寺。城南的双林寺，是元明清彩塑佛像的宝库。城北的镇国寺里，屹立着国内现存唯一的五代木结构建筑——万佛殿，雄浑古朴、构造精妙，见者无不叹服古人的匠心。

Located in central Shanxi, Pingyao Ancient City, also known as Tao in ancient times, was said to be a land conferred to Yao (c. 2200 BC, legendary Chinese sage king). First built in the Western Zhou Dynasty, it has nearly 4,000 buildings of the Ming and Qing dynasties. As the best-preserved ancient city in China, it deserves to be hailed as a typical representative of the Chinese civilization. After ascending the ancient town walls built during the years of Emperor Hongwu, you will see the gradual unfolding of a lively scroll of a county of the Ming and Qing dynasties. On the long and winding streets and alleys as dense as lines on a chessboard, exquisite and spacious mansions and courtyards are in disorderly profusion. The Southern Avenue on the central axis was the Chinese Wall Street at the end of the 19th century. With draft banks (19th century Shanxi banking institutions dealing in drafts or bills of exchange), private banks, pawnshops, cloth stores, pharmacies, and the like, the Southern Avenue was inclusive of almost all commercial professions in the Ming and Qing dynasties. In the final years of the Ming Dynasty, the businesses of the Shanxi merchants reached all corners of China, while wealthy and prominent merchants gathered in crowds in Pingyao. In 1823, Rishengchang (Daily Rising to Prosperity), the first draft bank in China, arose at an opportune time in Pingyao. With an increasing number of draft banks, Pingyao became China's financial center during that period. In 1997, together with two millennium-old temples outside the city, the ancient city was inscribed into the Representative List of the Intangible Cultural Heritage of Humanity. Located to the south of the city, the Shuanglin (Double Forests) Temple is a treasure-trove of the painted clay Buddhist statues in the Yuan (1271–1368), Ming, and Qing dynasties. In the Zhenguo (Nation-Pacifying) Temple to the north of the city stands the Wanfo (Ten Thousand Buddhas) Temple, the only wooden building from the Five Dynasties preserved in China. In this majestic, antiquely simplistic, and wonderfully structured temple, visitors cannot help marveling at the ingenuity of the ancients.

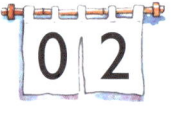

02 碛口：黄河古渡，龙吟碛口
Qikou: Ancient Ferry Crossing with Dragons' Chanting

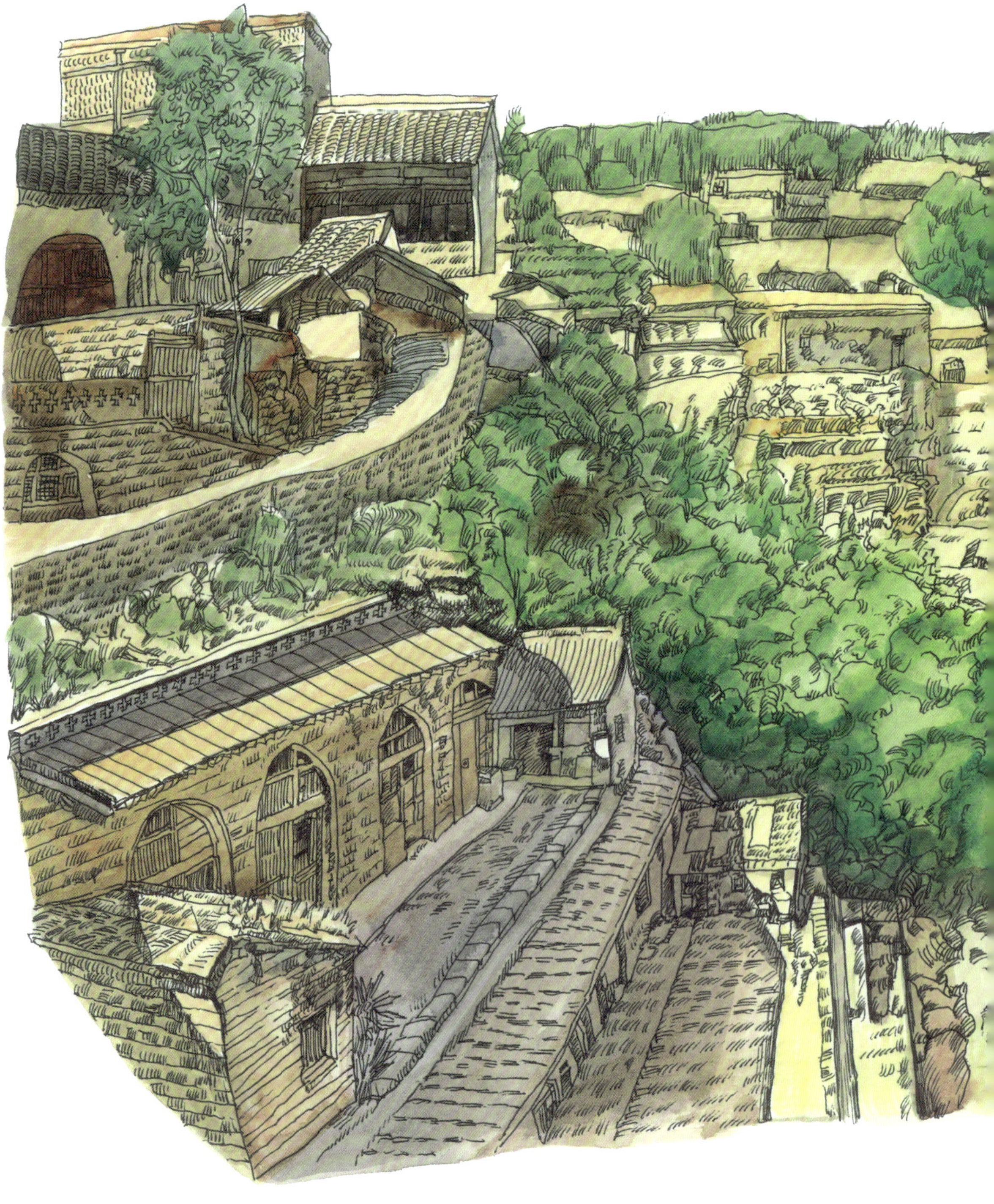

碛口位于晋陕峡谷中部，黄河、湫水在此交汇，卧虎山横亘其北。古镇河声岳色、阴阳和合，因紧靠黄河第二碛"大同碛"而得名。大同碛虎啸龙吟，其险无比，黄河漕运至此不得不转为陆运，碛口因此成为"水旱码头小都会，九曲黄河第一镇"，享有明末至民国三百多年富庶繁华的流金岁月。当年熙来攘往的码头、商肆和气势不凡的庙宇、民居等，大多被完好保存下来，走在镇上，仿佛时空凝固。巍然耸立山腰的黑龙庙是古镇地标，在庙对面的是戏台唱戏，黄河对岸的陕西也能听到。离古镇不远就是备受画家吴冠中推崇的李家山，还有西湾、孙家沟等古村，村中大多是碛口商人的家族院落。层层叠叠的窑洞大厦与山势完美结合，错落分布于黄土高坡上，如同与世隔绝的桃花源。

Located in the central part of the Jin-Shan (Shanxi-Shaanxi) Valley, Qikou sees the intersection of the Yellow River and the Qiushui River. It has the Wohu (Crouching Tiger) Mountain lying across its north. The ancient town features the audio and visual landscape of the rivers and mountains in perfectly harmonizing Yin and Yang. It is named Qikou because of its adjacency to the "Datong Qi" (the Rock of Great Harmony), the second-largest one of its kind in the Yellow River. Here, the water is like roaring tigers and chanting dragons. It is so perilous that the transport of grain by water to the capital via the Yellow River had to be turned into transport by land. As a result, the Qikou turned itself into "a small metropolis with docks for land and water transport services and the first town along the nine-bend Yellow River", enjoying its golden years amid richness and prosperity in a course of three hundred years from the final years of the Ming Dynasty to the period of the Republic of China. The docks and stores buzzing with activities, the extraordinarily imposing temples and residential buildings, and others have been mostly well-preserved. Strolling in the town, you will feel that time and space have frozen here. The Heilong (Black Dragon) Temple, which towers at the mountainside, is a landmark of the ancient temple. On the opposite side of the temple is a theatrical stage, whose singing can reach Shaanxi on the other shore of the Yellow River. Not far from the ancient city is the Lijia Mountain which had been greatly praised by Wu Guanzhong (1919-2010, Chinese painter). Besides, there are Xiwan, Sunjiagou, and other ancient villages in which you can find the courtyards of the clans of merchants from Qikou. Rows of large cave dwellings are in a perfect combination of mountain features. Distributed in attractive disorder throughout the Loess Plateau, they are like hidden lands of peace and prosperity cut off from the rest of the world.

03 张壁：明堡暗道，星象奇村
Zhangbi: Open Castle with Secret Passages and Extraordinary Village Corresponding to Star Signs

张壁古堡位于山西介休东南二十里的绵山北麓，三面沟壑地势险要，自古是兵家必争之地。古堡在隋末始建时用于屯兵，金代形成村落，明清臻于繁盛，至今有大量明清建筑保存下来。"奎十六星，天之武库也"，古堡格局恰与二十八星宿之奎宿对应，是古人星象堪舆理论的完美体现。更令人称奇的是，古堡地下挖了长达三千米的三层暗道，布局暗合"六壬奇门"之术，呈立体网状结构，里面机关密布、攻守兼备，宛如一座小型城池。张壁的明清古建中，最为流光溢彩的就是屋顶的琉璃装饰。明代空王行祠廊下，有两通孔雀蓝底琉璃碑，碑文黑釉书写，碑额三色二龙戏珠，通体琉璃烧制，美不胜收，堪称稀世奇珍。

Zhangbi Ancient Castle is located on the northern foot of the Mianshan Mountain, twenty li southeast of Jiexiu, Shanxi. Featuring a strategic location with its three sides facing ravines, it has been a place contested by all strategists. The ancient castle was first built for stationing troops in the last years of the Sui Dynasty, formed into a village in the Jin Dynasty (1115–1234), and brought to its pinnacle in the Ming and Qing dynasties. A great number of buildings of the Ming and Qing dynasties have been preserved. "The sixteen stars of the Kui constellation are the armories of Heaven." With its layout corresponding to the Kui constellation of the twenty-eight mansions, the ancient castle is a perfect embodiment of the ancients' theory of using star signs for judging Fengshui geomantic omen. More surprisingly, in the underground of the ancient castle, there are three stories of secret passages with a total length of three kilometers. The pattern coincides with the art of magic skills of going invisible by using the six ren-headed Stem-Branch pairs. In a three-dimensional network structure, it is full of machine-operated traps for both attacking and defending purposes, turning itself into a small-scale city. Among the buildings of the Ming and Qing dynasties in Zhangbi, the most brilliant and vibrant elements are the ceramic glaze decorations on the rooftops. On the corridor of the Temporary Temple of Dharmagahanābhyudgata-rāja in the Ming Dynasty, there are two ceramic glaze steles with peacock blue bottoms, with the inscriptions in black glaze. On the top parts of the steles are tri-colored scrolls featuring two dragons playing a pearl. Fired with colored glaze in their entireties, they are of utmost beauty and worthy of being hailed as rarely seen curios.

04 静升：灵石江南，三晋大宅
Jingsheng: Great Mansions in Lingshi (Comparable to the Areas South of the Yangtze River) of Shanxi

静升古镇位于山西灵石县，东眺绵山、西望汾河，周边沟壑纵横、梯田接天，山明水秀，风景怡人，有"小江南"之名。古镇历史悠久、经济繁荣，为晋商发祥地之一，康乾盛世中被称为"晋中第一镇"。在存留至今的大量古建中，王家大院是中国明清民居建筑的集大成者，号称"三晋第一宅"。王家大院由著名的太原王氏后裔所建，包含五座庞大城堡，房屋上千间。其中高家崖和红门堡东西相望、一桥相连，建筑最富有特色。层楼叠院依山就势，木质建筑与窑洞完美融合。典雅精美、寓意丰富的木雕、石雕和砖雕使院落华光四射，意境悠远、端秀苍健的楹联增添儒雅书香之气。形似毛笔直指苍穹的文笔塔，历经数百年风雨沧桑仍巍巍屹立，象征着文脉不断、文思泉涌。红墙红门的红庙，颇为引人瞩目。每年6月的红庙庙会热闹非凡，各种民俗表演一应俱全，十分有趣。

Located in Lingshi County, Shanxi Province, Jingsheng Ancient Town faces Mianshan Mountain to its east and Fenhe River to its west. Surrounded by crisscrossing ravines and towering terraced fields, it has picturesque and pleasant scenery, earning itself the reputation of "Small Jiangnan (the areas south of the Yangtze River)". Featuring a time-honored history and a prosperous economy, it was one of the places of origin for the Shanxi merchants. It was hailed as "the first town in central Shanxi" in the Kangxi-Qianlong Great Ages (1662–1796). Among the great number of ancient buildings preserved, the Wang Family Compound, which is an epitome of the residential buildings of the Ming and Qing dynasties in China, has been reputed as "the first compound in Shanxi". Built by the descendants of the famous Wang Clan in Taiyuan, the Wang Family Compound contains five large-scale castles and over 1,000 rooms. Among them, the Gaojiaya Castle and the Hongmen Castle, which face each other on the east-west line, are connected by a bridge, with each of them manifesting the most distinctive architectural features. The multi-storied buildings and the multi-folded courtyards follow the mountain features, with the wooden buildings in a perfect combination with the cave dwellings. Various wood, stone, and brick carvings, which are refined, elegant, and exquisite, add radiance to the courtyards. The couplets, featuring profound artistic conception and writing strokes either in beautiful or robust styles, bestow an ambiance of elegance and literary flavor. In the shape of a writing brush rising abruptly towards the sky, the Wenbi (Write Brush) Pagoda has been towering after enduring centuries of the elements, as a symbol of the uninterrupted cultural lineage and the gushing ideas in writing. The Hongmiao (Red) Temple, characterized by its red walls and red gate, is attracting the gaze of the people. In June every year, the temple fair there presents scenes of bustle and excitement, with assorted interesting popular custom performances.

陕西
Shaanxi

党家村：民居瑰宝，不染纤尘
Dangjia Village: Treasure of Residential Buildings Without a Speck of Dust

陕西韩城党家村，隐藏于黄河西岸的泌水河谷中。村落始建于元代，主要有党、贾两姓。经过明清富商大族持续兴建，成为一个看家楼、私塾、戏楼、庙宇、古井、涝池等一应俱全的皇皇大村。至今村中仍保存有一百二十三座四合院，十一座祠堂，还有文星阁、节孝碑等精美的明清建筑。走进党家村，轩敞的四合院鳞次栉比，青砖青瓦纤尘不染，走马门楼高大气派，楹联门楣端秀雅致，精美三雕俯拾即是。最令人称奇的是，这些院落历经数百年风霜仍光洁如新，置身其中仿佛穿越了时空。相传这缘于文星阁中藏有一颗避尘珠，实际上是因为党家村选址高明，背山面水，浮尘极少，河谷的存在又减缓了风势。独具匠心的水道设计使雨水从院落流入青石巷道，再汇入泌水河，如此村中雨天不仅无泥，还更加清洁。古老的建筑中融入了党家村先人的风水智慧、人文情怀和无限希冀，不愧是"世界民居之瑰宝"。

Located in Hancheng of Shaanxi Province, Dangjia Village looms in the Mishui River valley on the western bank of Yellow River. First built in the Yuan Dynasty, the village mostly consists of the people surnamed Dang and Jia. Expanded by wealthy merchants and influential clans in the Ming and Qing dynasties, it has been a brilliant village incorporating watchtowers, private schools, stage buildings, temples, ancient wells, floodwater ponds, and others. Preserved in the village are 123 quadrangle courtyards, 11 temples, and exquisite buildings of the Ming and Qing dynasties such as the Wenxing (Cultural Star) Pavilion and the Jiexiao (Integrity and Filial Piety) Monument. After entering the Dangjia Village, you will see the spacious quadrangle courtyards in tight rows, with spotless green bricks and tiles, imposing gateway arches higher than horse-riders, beautiful, elegant, and exquisite couplets and horizontal scrolls on lintels, and common and exquisite "triple carvings". More surprisingly, after centuries of enduring the elements, these courtyards are still as bright and clean as if they were newly built, in which you feel like that you have traveled through time and space. It is said that it is due to the Dust-Repelling Pearl in the Cultural Star Pavilion. In fact, it is because the Dangjia Village was built on a favorably chosen location with mountains at the back and a river in front which bring little dust. Besides, the river valley slows down the wind. The waterways designed with ingenuity cause the rainwater to flow from courtyards into the tunnels built with green rocks and then to converge into the Mishui River. As a result, on rainy days, the village is not only free from mud but even cleaner. The ancient buildings have been imbued with the ancestors' wisdom of geomancy, humanistic feelings, and infinite hopes. The village lives up to its reputation of being "a treasure among residential buildings in the world".

06 青木川：山中桃源，乱世传奇
Qingmuchuan: Mountainous Land of Peace and Prosperity with a Legend During Turbulent Days

　　青木川隶属陕西宁强县，在青山环抱中，古镇形似游龙伏于金溪河两岸。青木川始建于明中叶，民国时成为陕、甘、川三省交会的要冲和名振三边的商贸重镇。在战火纷扰的乱世中，青木川却能成为物阜民丰的山中桃源，主要得益于当年称雄一方的传奇人物魏辅唐。他是从叶广芩小说《青木川》改编的电视剧《一代枭雄》中的主角原型。以他命名的辅唐宴，如今成了当地招牌菜。在明代沿河而建的回龙场老街上，古色古香的商行店铺林立。那中西合璧的洋房子，雕栏玉砌的旱船屋，曲屏深院的大烟馆，都是当年魏氏家族的产业。雄踞山坡的辅仁中学今天仍书声琅琅，最初亦由魏氏出资修建，学堂不收学费，课程设计先进，培育了不少英才。走进朱扉高牖、轩峻壮丽的魏氏宅院，一曲惊心动魄的乱世传奇在心中回荡。

　　Qingmuchuan is under the jurisdiction of Ningqiang County, Shaanxi Province. Embraced by mountains, the ancient town lies prostrate like a meandering dragon on both banks of the Jinxi River. First built in the middle of the Ming Dynasty, Qingmuchuan became a strategic intersection of Shaanxi, Gansu, and Sichuan and a significant commerce and trade tower reputable throughout Sanbian (Dingbian, Anbian, and Jingbian in northern Shaanxi Province). During the turbulent days enveloped in the flames of war, Qingmuchuan became a mountainous land of peace and prosperity where products abounded and the people lived in plenty. It should be mostly credited to Wei Tangfu (1902–1952), a legendary figure holding sway over the region during that period. He was the archetype of the protagonist in the TV series *A Hero* adapted from the novel titled *Qingmuchuan* written by Ye Guangqin (1948–, Chinese writer). The Futang Banquet named after him has become a local brand with signature dishes offered at present. On the Huilongchang Ancient Street built along the River in the Ming Dynasty, shops and stores with antique appeal stand in great numbers. Properties such as the Western-style houses, the land boat dwellings with carved balustrades and marble steps, the opium shops with screen walls, and deep courtyards belonged to the Wei Clan back then. The Furen Middle School, towering on the mountainside, is still used at present. Funded by the Wei Clan to be built, the school did not charge for tuition. With its advanced curriculum, it has cultivated a number of talents. After entering the mansion of the Wei Clan featuring crimson gates, high lattice windows, and other elements amid its spaciousness and magnificence, you will feel a soul-stirring legend during turbulent days.

北京
Beijing

07 爨底下：京西山村，北国幽谷
Cuandixia: Mountainous Village in the West of Beijing and a Secluded Valley of Northern China

爨底下村卧于北京西郊门头沟的深山峡谷中，因建于明朝关隘爨里口的下方而得名。古村始建于明永乐年间，村民皆是当年戍守爨里口的韩氏三兄弟的后裔。明正德年间修建的古驿道，使这里成为过往客商落脚的重要驿站。登高俯瞰，只见群山环抱中，七十余座精巧的清代四合院依山就势，高低错落卧于缓坡之上。沿蜿蜒小巷走进村里，阳光下紫石、青石、灰石铺砌的路面色彩迷人。伫立百余年的四合院古朴大气、建造精良。墙体磨砖对缝，屋宇雕梁画栋。建在最高处的财主院，装饰也最为讲究。门口铺砌两块石板，青石寓意"脚踏青云"，紫石寓意"紫气东来"。距古村不远有一处天险奇观，是一段长达百余米的天然侵蚀峡谷，幽远深邃、峭壁参天，人称"一线天"，许多影视剧在这里取过景，比如电影《投名状》。

The Cuandixia Village, perched in the ravine of the deep mountains in Mentougou, the western suburbs of Beijing, is named for its location under the Cuanlikou mountain pass of the Ming Dynasty. First built during the years of Emperor Yongle (r. 1403–1414), the village was dwelled by the descendants of the three brothers of the Han family who guarded Cuanlikou. The ancient post road built during the years of Emperor Zhengde (1505–1521) of the Ming Dynasty enabled this place to be a significant post station for traveling merchants. You may ascend to a height and look down to see over 70 quadrangle courtyards exquisitely constructed in line with the mountain features and lying prostrate in attractive disorder on the gentle slopes. Following the meandering alleys into the village, you will see the colorful and appealing road surfaces paved with purple rocks, green rocks, and grey rocks under the sunshine. The quadrangles, which have been standing for centuries, are antiquely simplistic and delicately built. The walls feature well-joined polished bricks while the buildings are richly ornamented. The Rich Master Courtyard, which is built at the highest place, is characterized by mostly particular decorations. Among the two stone slabs paved at the entrance, the green slab means "stepping on a position as high as clouds with feet", while the purple slab symbolizes "the propitious purple air coming from the east". No far from the ancient village is a marvelous spectacle of a natural barrier, which is a naturally corroded valley with a length of hundreds of meters. Secluded and deep with cliffs reaching high into the sky, it has been known as "a thin strip of the sky" and used as a shooting site for many movies and TV shows such as the movie titled *The Warlords*.

河北
Hebei

 鸡鸣驿：塞北邮驿，古道沧桑
Jimingyi: Post Station Beyond the Great Wall
with Ancient Roads of Vicissitudes

鸡鸣驿隶属河北张家口怀来县，因背靠雄伟的鸡鸣山而得名，是现存最完整的一座驿站古城。驿站始建于元代，明代扩建为西北往来京城的第一大站，城内驿丞署、驿仓、公馆、马号等一应俱全。邮驿的发展带动了小城的全面繁荣，明清两朝这里商贾云集、店铺林立，馆阁宏伟、庙宇堂皇，是人烟鼎盛的塞北重镇。历经五百年风雨的城墙如今仍巍然屹立，从苍凉破败的城楼远眺，古老的驿道笔直宽阔，当年飞马传驿、烟尘滚滚的情景如在目前。城西北的明代公馆仍保存完好，栩栩如生的木雕令人称叹。前街上的贺家大院，过去是驿丞署。当年八国联军入侵北京，慈禧太后仓皇西逃，就曾下榻此处。大院山墙上"鸿禧接福"四字，暗含着这段隐秘的历史。

Jimingyi, which is under the jurisdiction of Huailai County, Zhangjiakou, Hebei Province, is named after the majestic Jiming (Cock's Crowing) Mountain at its back. It is the best-preserved post station and ancient city. First built in the Yuan Dynasty, it was expanded into the largest post station on the journey between the northwest and the capital in the Ming Dynasty. The post station is well furnished with the post station superintendent mansion, the post station warehouse, the residential quarters, the stables, and others. The development of the post station had driven the full prosperity of the small city. During the Ming and Qing dynasties, it witnessed merchants gathering in crowds and shops and stores in great numbers. With its grand halls and pavilions and magnificent temples, it was a strategic town at the height of power and splendor beyond the Great Wall. After five centuries of enduring natural elements, the city walls are still erect. Looking into the distance from the dilapidated gate tower, you will see the straight and wide post roads, as if laying eyes on the scenes of galloping horses to relate messages amid the billowy dust. In the northwest of the city are the well-preserved living quarters from the Ming Dynasty, where the life-like wooden carvings draw great admirations. On Front Street is the He Clan Courtyard, which was the post station superintendent mansion. When the Eight-Power Allied Forces invaded Beijing in 1900, Empress Dowager Cixi (1835–1908, regent 1861–1908) fled westward in a flurry and settled at this site. The inscriptions of Hongxi Jiefu (tremendous auspiciousness in receiving good fortune) on the gable of the courtyard imply this hidden historical period.

09 暖泉镇：古堡金花，逢源暖泉
Nuanquan Town: Golden Flowers in an Antique Castle with Smoothly Flowing Warm Spring Water

河北蔚县暖泉镇，始建于元代，因村中有一处三东不冻的清泉而得名。明清时期暖泉发展为"三堡、六巷、十八庄"，成为蔚县西部的交通枢纽和商贸重镇。岁月流转，大地上繁华和苍凉此起彼伏。喧嚣远去，建筑却得以保存，成为凝固的历史。始建于明嘉靖年间的西古堡，集城堡、戏楼、庙宇、宅院于一体，兼具居住和军事防御功能，保存最为完好，建筑最为独特。那高大气派的门楼、连环相套的院落、前廊后厦的格局和雕绘精美的装饰，无不透露出昔日的富庶繁华。清雅的暖泉书院是元代工部尚书王敏的家塾，暖泉便是从书院中的逢源池出水，绕村缓流。打树花是暖泉人传承三百余年的绝技，表演时将熔化的铁水泼洒到古老的城墙上，火花迸溅，如一树金色繁花绽放撒落，美得惊心动魄。

Located in Yuxian County of Hebei Province, Nuanquan (Warm Spring) Town was first built in the Yuan Dynasty. It was named after a clear spring which is non-freezable even on the coldest days each year in the village. During the Ming and Qing dynasties, it was developed into "three castles, six valleys, and eighteen villages", when it became a transportation junction and a significant business and trade town in the west of Yuxian County. Over time, the land has experienced ups and downs. As all the hustle and bustle faded away, the buildings have been preserved as solidified history. The West Ancient Castle, built during the years of Emperor Jiajing (1522–1566), can also be used as a castle, stage building, temple, and living building, for both living and defending. It features the best preservation and the most unique building style. Its elements, such as the imposing gateway arch, the connected courtyards, the layout with front porches before buildings, and the exquisitely carved decorations, reveals its richness and prosperity in the past. The Nuanquan (Warm Spring) Academy, featuring a refined and elegant ambiance, was the family school of Wang Min (around the 14th century), Minister of Public Works in the Yuan Dynasty. The warm spring water flows from the Fengyuan (Smoothly Flowing) Pool of the academy to slowly circulate the village. It has been a unique skill of the people of Nuanquan to present "tree flowers" for three centuries. During a performance, the molten iron is splashed onto the ancient city walls, causing sparks to splatter like a whole tree of flowers blooming and falling. It is thrillingly beautiful.

河南
Henan

 朱仙镇：中原名镇，忠义相传
Zhuxian Town: Famous Town in the Central Plains with the Transmission of Loyalty and Righteousness

朱仙镇位于河南开封市西南郊，春秋时期已成民居聚落。借贾鲁河漕运之利，明清两朝臻于鼎盛，码头帆樯林立、城中商贾云集，富庶繁华位居当时"中国四大名镇"之首。古镇原名聚仙镇，后因"窃符救赵"的战国义士朱亥封于此地，改称朱仙镇。"纵死侠骨香，不惭世上英"，朱亥是朱仙镇人心中的英雄，是千年古镇忠义根脉的源头所在。这里也曾是岳飞第四次北伐的最后一站，当年岳飞点将的高台依旧挺立，朱仙镇大捷成为人人耳熟能详的英雄传奇。庄严恢宏、碑亭林立的岳飞庙屹立数百年，每年古镇入伍的新兵都会来这里举行拜别仪式，将岳飞精忠报国的精神世代相承。朱仙镇还是豫剧和木版年画的发祥地，来到这里一定要听一听荡气回肠的豫剧祥符调，赏一赏明艳生动的朱仙镇木版年画。

Located in a southwestern suburb of Kaifeng City, Henan Province, Zhuxian (Immortal Zhu) Town had become a local settlement during the Spring and Autumn period (770–476). With the advantages of the transport of grain via the Jialu River to the capital, it reached its height of power and splendor during the Ming and Qing dynasties. With a forest of masts in its wharves and an assemblage of merchants in the city, it was "the top one among the four major Chinese towns" in terms of its richness and prosperity. Originally known as the Juxian (Immortal-Gathering) Town, it was renamed Zhuxian Town for being a land conferred to Zhu Hai (around the third century BC), a high-minded and righteous person during the Warring States period (475–221 BC) who "stole a seal to save the Zhao state". "Even in his death, his bones of chivalry are still fragrant, living up to his heroic reputation when he was alive." Zhu Hai, a hero of Zhuxian Town, has been the source of loyalty and righteousness of this millennium-old ancient town. The town was also the last stop of Yue Fei (1103–1142, an ancient Chinese patriot and general) during his fourth northern expedition. The high platform on which Yue Fei called the muster roll of generals and assigned them tasks is still towering. The Great Victory of the Zhuxian Town (1140) has been a heroic legend familiar to every head here. Yue Fei's Temple, with a great number of stele pavilions amid its solemn and grand ambiance, has been erect for centuries. Every year, the new army recruits from the ancient town come here to attend a farewell ceremony, passing on Yue Fei's spirit of serving China with unreserved loyalty. Zhuxian Town is also the cradle of Henan Opera and woodblock New Year pictures. During your visit here, you are recommended to listen to the heart-rending Xiangfu tunes of Henan Opera and admire the bright and vivid woodblock New Year pictures of Zhuxian Town.

# 赊店镇：皇城气派，铁旗商魂
Shedian Town: the Demeanor of an Imperial City and the Merchants' Soul with Iron-Firm Flags

河南南阳赊店镇坐落于伏牛山南麓，潘河、赵河交汇处。古镇历史悠久，相传因汉光武帝刘秀曾在此地赊酒旗起兵而得名。为报赊旗的情义，刘秀称帝后还赐赊店享皇城同等建制，设九座城门。赊店老酒也因此远近扬名，至今畅销不衰。赊店三面环水，明清时期作为南北水陆交通的枢纽，曾有数百年流金岁月。将茶叶远销俄国的著名晋商常万达，就曾在赊店设立茶庄分号，作为万里茶路上的水陆货运中转站。繁华远逝，昔日的辉煌凝固在古镇幢幢碧瓦飞甍的清代建筑中。青砖灰瓦的瓷器街上商肆林立，广盛镖局、蔚盛长票号、厘金局门口猎猎飘动的旗帜，似在诉说荣耀往事。地处闹市中心的山陕会馆，以规模之宏大严整、建筑之富丽华美，荣膺"中国第一会馆"之名。会馆中"诚信赢天下"的匾额和"大义参天"的铁旗杆，传递着晋商"诚信为本、以义取利"的经商理念。

Shedian Town is located at the junction of the Panhe River and the Zhaohe River on the southern foot of the Funiu Mountain, Nanyang, Henan Province. The ancient town features a time-honored history. It is said that the Shedian (Credit Store) Town got its name because of Liu Xiu, later Emperor Guangwu (r. 25–57) of the Han Dynasty, who brought flags and wine on credit here to stage an armed rebellion. To repay the kindness of buying banners on credit, Liu Xiu, after claiming himself emperor, decreed that Shedian Town shared the equal architectural structure with that of the imperial capital with nine gates. The wine of Shedian Town, with its reputation spreading far and wide, is still in great demand at present. With its three sides facing the water, Shedian Town was a water and land traffic hub between the north and the south during the Ming and Qing dynasties, enjoying centuries of prosperity. Chang Wanda, a famous Shanxi merchant who sold tea leaves to Russia, set up a branch of his tea shops in Shedian as water and land transfer station on the tea road stretching for over ten thousand li. As prosperity faded, the past glories have been solidified in the buildings of the Qing Dynasty with their green tiles and overhanging eaves. On the porcelain streets with green bricks and grey tiles, the fluttering banners before the Guangsheng Biaoju (a commercial firm for providing armed escorts or

bodyguards), the Weishengchang Draft Bank (a 19th-century Shanxi banking institution dealing in drafts or bills of exchange), and the Lijin (provincial transit duty) Bureau seem to be telling the past matters of glory. The Shanxi–Shaanxi Guildhall, which is located in the downtown of the ancient town, has been hailed as "the First Guildhall in China" with its grand and well-organized scale and magnificent buildings. In the guild are the horizontal scroll of "credibility winning over the country" and the iron-pole banner of "great righteousness reaching high to the sky", which convey the business concept of "taking credibility as the roots and seeking gain with righteousness".

山东
Shandong

新城镇：半朝王家，四世宫保
Xincheng Town: Filling Half of the Imperial Court with the Wang Clan Members, with the Fourth-Generation Imperial Protector

新城镇隶属山东淄博桓台县，春秋时期这一带是齐国苑囿，因境内有齐桓公戏马高台，桓台县由此得名。新城自古文运昌隆，明清两朝出过七十二位进士，仕宦百余人，皆有廉名。明万历年间，新城王家同朝为官者达三十余人，时人谓之"半朝王家"。雄峙四百余年的"四世宫保"牌坊，就是万历皇帝为表彰时任兵部尚书的王象乾而特许建造的。王象乾威震九边、守国有功，万历皇帝追封他祖上三代皆为"光禄大夫柱国太子太保兵部尚书"。臻于荣耀巅峰的王家，给后世留下了这座庄严华美的"华夏第一砖坊"。牌坊为砖石结构，顶部飞檐斗拱，四角杵头兽面，浮雕生动精美，瓦脊中"麒麟驮宝瓶"的雕饰尤为独特。匾额上"四世宫保"四个大字端严道劲，是书法大家董其昌的手笔。清朝"一代诗宗"王士祯亦出自新城王家，故居今日犹在，诗词千载传咏。祖辈的读书之风、廉正之风，在新城世代相传。

Under the jurisdiction of Huantai County, Zibo, Shandong Province, Xincheng Town was a hunting ground of the Qi State during the Spring and Autumn period (770-476 BC). The name of Huantai County came from the *Tai* (high platform) where Duke Huan of Qi (r. 685–643) rode horses. With its prosperous cultural lineage since ancient times, Xincheng witnessed the emergence of seventy-two successful candidates of the imperial civil examinations of the highest level during the Ming and Qing dynasties and hundreds of officials, with all of them being honest and incorruptible. During the years of Wanli (1573–1619), more than 30 members of the Wang Clan in Xincheng were serving as officials in the imperial court at the same time, earning the renowned notion of "filling half of the imperial court with members of the Wang's Clan". The memorial arch of "the fourth-generation imperial protector" which has been erected for over four centuries was built under a special decree of Emperor Wanli (r. 1573–1620) of the Ming Dynasty to commend Wang Xiangqian (1546–1630), the Minister of War during the years of Wanli. With Wang Xiangqian's mighty name on frontiers and meritorious services in safeguarding the country, the emperor conferred posthumous titles to the latest three generations of his ancestors as "Grand Masters for Splendid Happiness, Pillars of the State, Grand Guardians of the Heir Apparent, and Ministers of War". The Wang's Clan, reaching its pinnacle of glory, left this solemn and magnificent "No.1 brick memorial arch of China" to future generations. With a masonry structure, the memorial arch features overhanging eaves and Dougong (corbel brackets) on its top, animal faces with poking heads on its four corners, and vivid and exquisite bas-relief. The carvings of the "kirin carrying a treasure vase on its back" on the roof tile are the most unique. The inscriptions of "the fourth-generation imperial protector" on the horizontal scroll, which are regular, rigorous, and vigorous, were produced by Dong Qichang (1555–1637, ancient Chinese calligrapher). Wang Shizhen (1634–1711), hailed as "dean of poets among his contemporaries" in the Qing dynasties, was also from the Wang Clan in Xincheng. His former residence was still there, while his poems have been passed on for millennia. The customs of reading and remaining incorruptible have been passed on from generation to generation in Xincheng.

第七章
Chapter 7

岭南风情
Local Conditions and Customs of the South of the Five Ridges

广西
Gangxi

01 兴坪：奇山秀水，景甲天下
Xingping: Beautiful Mountains and Rivers amid Its Best Landscape in China

兴坪古镇隶属广西桂林阳朔县，拥有漓江沿岸最美的一段风景。三国时东吴曾在此地设熙平县治，如今在其遗址上，古砖瓦陶瓷残片仍随处可见。在这座有一千七百多年历史的古镇里，保存最完整的古建筑是一座乾隆年间修建的戏台。台缘横贯着四出传统戏曲木制浮雕图，人物栩栩如生。世人皆知"桂林山水甲天下"，却不知其山水精华尽在兴坪。晨起泛舟漓江，江水清平如镜，两岸群峰倒映、翠竹成林，舟行至九马画山，只见石壁如屏、五彩斑驳，似有九马隐于画屏中，造化神奇如天公醉笔。顺流南下至黄布滩，米黄巨石映在一曲清江中，似黄布铺于水中。黄布滩两岸，有七座秀美山峰，似仙子出浴，被称作"七仙女下凡"。兴坪秀甲天下的山水，还被印在了贰拾元人民币上。许多游人到这里，都会拍一张与人民币背景图同款的风景照，把这奇山秀水永远留住。

Under the jurisdiction of Yangshuo, Guilin of Guangxi, Xingping Ancient Town has the most beautiful scenery of the Lijiang River. The county seat of Xiping County was set up here by the Eastern Wu State (229–280) during the Three Kingdoms period. Scraps of ancient bricks, tiles, and porcelain are still seen everywhere on the historical site. In this ancient town with a history of over 1,700 years, the best-preserved ancient building is a stage built in the years of Emperor Qianlong. On the sides of the stage are four wooden relief drawings featuring traditional operas with vivid figures. It is widely known that "Guilin's landscape is the best in the world", but few had the idea that the essence of Guilin's landscape is in Xingping. In the morning, you may go boating on the Lijiang River where the river water is as clear and tranquil as a mirror reflecting peaks on both banks lined with forests of emerald bamboos. When the boat reaches the scenic spot of A Painting of Nine Horses on a Mountain, you will see that the stone cliff is like a multi-colored screen, as if having nine horses on it. The miraculous moves of Nature are like the painting strokes of the Heavenly Emperor in his drinking ecstasy. You may follow the river to go downstream southward to reach the Huangbu (Yellow Cloth) Beach, where a rice-yellow huge rock is reflected on the clear river as if having a stretch of yellow cloth spread on the water. On both banks of the Yellow Cloth Beach are seven elegant and beautiful peaks that look like fairies who have just taken a bath. They are hailed as "seven fairies who descended to the human world". Xingping's landscape which ranks first in the world is printed on the 20 Chinese Yuan banknote. Here, many visitors will take a landscape photo of the scenery, which is the same as the background of the banknote, intending to keep this beautiful landscape forever.

02 黄姚：千年诗集，梦境家园
Huangyao: A Millennium-Old Poetry Collection amid a Dreamlike Home

广西贺州黄姚古镇隐于南岭余脉中，四周九峰环绕、三溪汇流，风水奇佳。古镇发祥于宋，兴盛于明清，因远离尘嚣至今古貌犹存。镇外岩溶遍布、峰丛耸立，是典型的喀斯特地貌，镇内亭台楼阁掩映于古榕翠竹间，按九宫八卦布局的屋舍与山水融为一体，美如出园梦境。黄姚"有山必有水，有水必有桥，有桥必有亭，有亭必有联，有联必有匾"，诗情画意处处流淌，宛如一部静置千年的诗集。走入古镇，三百余幢明清建筑错落分布于八条阡陌纵横的青石街巷中，飞檐翘角的明代古戏台伫立在湍急的姚江边，数百年的悲欢离合随水而逝。黄姚有十五座古桥梁，以明朝带龙桥最美。双拱如半月弯于溪水上，电影《面纱》就曾在此取景。溪边的龙爪榕盘根错节如巨龙汲水，汇聚八百多年天地灵气，护佑一方。流淌数百年的仙人古井，泉水始终不盈不亏，五座方池分工巧妙，沿用至今。

Looming in the stretching branch of Nanling Mountain, Hezhou, Guangxi, Huangyao Ancient Town is surrounded by nine peaks and three streams, featuring extremely favorable geomancy. The ancient town was established in the Song Dynasty and came to its pinnacle in the Ming and Qing dynasties. Its location, far from the madding crowd, enables the preservation of its ancient features. Beyond the town, there are commonly seen karsts and towering peaks, indicating a typical karst landform. Inside the town, various buildings, including pavilions, terraces, and towers, loom amid ancient banyan trees and emerald trees. The buildings, arranged according to the traditional Chinese theory of nine palaces and eight trigrams, merge with the landscape, presenting an idyllic dreamland. In Huangyao, "such elements as mountains, water, bridges, pavilions, couplets, and horizontal scrolls are often found in co-existence", with poetic charm revealed in each spot, turning it into a millennium-old poetry collection in its tranquility. After entering the ancient town, you will see over 300 buildings of the Ming and Qing dynasties distributed in attractive disorder on eight crisscrossing streets and alleys paved with green slabs. The ancient stage with its overhanging eaves and cornices, which was built in the Ming Dynasty, stands on the shore of the torrential Yaojiang River, witnessing centuries of ups and downs fading away with the flowing water. Among the fifteen ancient bridges of Huangyao, the Dailong (Dragon-Girding) Bridge is the most beautiful one. With its dual arches, it stretches like a crescent over the stream. It was the shooting ground for some scenes of the movie titled *The Painted Veil*. Beside the stream is the Longzhua (Dragon Claws) Banyan. With its twisted roots and gnarled branches, it looks like a dragon drawing water. Having converged the pneuma of Heaven and Earth for over eight hundred years, it has been safeguarding the local area. The Ancient Well of Immortals, which has been flowing for centuries, has been full of water, neither brimming nor draining. With five square pools in an ingenious division of labor, it is still used at present.

03 扬美：左江明珠，融汇南北
Yangmei: A Bright Pearl Beside the Zuojiang River, Fusing the South and the North

广西南宁扬美古镇地处左江下游，三面环江、水清见底，江畔古木参天、奇石嶙峋，险秀风景曾得徐霞客盛赞。古镇始建于宋，因水运兴于明清，至民国仍是百货辐辏的繁华商埠。依左江岸边台地而建的临江街，当年车马如龙，如今唯余静静伫立的明清老屋，那飞檐青脊、柱础石雕，仍透露出昔日荣华。由七根木柱连成屋架的七柱屋简洁舒朗、冬暖夏凉，已历经四百余年风霜。扬美人的先祖多来自山东，北宋时随狄青平蛮南下迁居于此，也把儒家文化带了过来，明清两朝扬美出过六个进士、四个举人。建于乾隆元年的魁星楼形似"帝印"，是辛亥革命的重要纪念地。五叠堂建于清嘉庆年间，五进院落一进比一进高，寓意步步高升。整体看建筑四平八稳，既传承了庄重典雅的齐鲁风格，也融汇了细腻秀丽的岭南特色。南北交融的建筑文化体现了扬美古镇独特的人文之美。

Located in the lower reaches of the Zuojiang River, Nanning, Guangxi, Yangmei Ancient Town is surrounded on three sides by the river with its bottom revealed by clear water. The river's banks are lined with towering ancient trees and craggy rocks. Its beautiful landscape was highly praised by Xu Xiake (1587–1641, an ancient Chinese travel writer and geographer, author of *Xu Xiake's Travel Diaries*). First built during the Song Dynasty, it prospered in the Ming and Qing dynasties. In the period of the Republic of China, it was still a flourishing commercial port with converged goods. Built on the tableland on the bank of the Zuojiang River, the Linjiang (River-Adjacent) Street witnessed bustling vehicles and horses in history and has ancient buildings of the Ming and Qing dynasties standing in tranquility. With their overhanging eaves, green ridges, plinths, and stone carvings, they still reveal the past glories. The Qizhu (Seven Pillars) Building, with seven wooden pillars linked to form its frame, is simplistic, relaxing, and bright, making it warm in winter and cool in summer. It has endured over four centuries of elements. Ancestors of the people of Yangmei were mostly from Shandong Province. During the Northern Song Dynasty, they followed Di Qing (1008–1057, an ancient Chinese general) on his southward expedition against barbarian enemies and settled down here. They also brought Confucian culture here and witnessed the emergence of six successful candidates of the imperial civil examination at the highest level and four at the provincial level. The Kuixing (four stars in the bowl of the Big Dipper, believed to be gods presiding over literature and writing) Building, which was built in the first year of Emperor Qianlong, is a significant commemorative site of the Xinhai Revolution in 1911 (which ended the feudal rule in China). The Wudie (Five Folds) Hall, which was built during the years of Emperor Jiaqing, features five courtyards, with each higher than the one before it, implying a steady rise. Judged from its wholeness, the building is well-balanced, having inherited the solemn, refined, and elegant style of Shandong and the exquisite features of the south of the Five Ridges. Its architectural culture blending the south and the north has embodied the unique humanistic beauty of the Yangmei Ancient Town.

广东
Guangdong

04 赤坎：中西合璧，古埠侨乡
Chikan: Ancient Commercial Port and Hometown of Overseas Chinese with an Integration of Chinese and Western Elements

赤坎古镇坐落于广东开平市中部的潭江之滨，开埠于清顺治年间，因水运便利成为繁华商埠。赤坎还是著名的侨乡，衣锦荣归的华侨把异域风情带回故里，造就了中西合璧、千姿百态的侨乡建筑群。在赤坎六百余座骑楼中，以堤西路一带最壮观，沿河畔连绵数里，罗马石柱、彩格窗、巴洛克风格的山花与传统骑楼结合得天衣无缝。古老的招牌、斑驳的墙面，行走其间仿佛穿越到民国电影中。碉楼是赤坎另一特色，其中以建于明嘉靖朝的迎龙楼最为古老，代表了开平碉楼的原始形态。地势险要的南楼是当年司徒氏七烈士坚守抗日的据点，见证着侨乡人的铁血丹心。司徒氏和关氏两大家族的图书馆，恢宏壮美，是赤坎最具特色的建筑，诉说着两大家族的百年兴衰浮沉。

Located on the bank of Tanjiang River in central Kaiping City, Guangdong, Chikan Ancient Town began as a wharf during the years of Emperor Shunzhi in the Qing Dynasty. With its convenient waterborne transport, it became a prosperous commercial port. Chikan has been a famous hometown of overseas Chinese. They have returned with their acquired wealth and honor and brought the alien conditions and customs back to their hometown, giving rise to clusters of buildings featuring Chinese and Western elements and various styles in this hometown of overseas Chinese. Among over six hundred arcade buildings in Chikan, those on the Tixi Road are the most spectacular. They stretch along the bank for several miles. The Roman stone pillars, the color-check windows, and the Baroque pediments have integrated seamlessly with the traditional arcade buildings. Sauntering beside the ancient signboards and the mottled walls, you seem to be traveling through time and space back to the period of the Republic of China as depicted in movies. Chikan is also featured by watchtowers. Among them is the Yinglong (Dragon-Greeting) Building, the oldest one which was built during the years of Emperor Jiajing of the Ming Dynasty. It represents the primitive form of Kaiping Diaolou (Watchtowers) buildings. The Nanlou (South) Building, which is strategically situated and easy to defend, was a stronghold of the seven martyrs of the Situ Clan to hold fast to resist the Japanese aggression, being a testament to the iron will and patriotism of the overseas Chinese. Majestic and beautiful, the libraries of the Situ Clan and the Guan Clan are the most distinctively featured buildings in Chikan, telling centuries of ups and downs of the two prestigious clans.

05 沙湾：金声玉振，飘色粤韵
Shawan: Land of Piaose Art Featuring Guangdong's Appeal and Sounds of Gold and Jade

沙湾古镇位于广州市番禺区，始建于南宋，原为古海湾，经历代筑堤围垦渐成陆地，明清时期已是"烟火万家"。顺着青石街巷走入古镇，首先映入眼帘的是一道道流丽高耸的镬耳墙，极具广府特色。镬耳形如官帽，寓意"独占鳌头"，过去是地位和财富的象征。无数气派的镬耳大屋透露着沙湾昔日荣华，而更匠心独运的是富有雕塑感的蚝壳墙。用蚝壳砌墙不仅坚固美观，还防水防虫、冬暖夏凉。古镇居民大多姓何，宏大肃穆的留耕堂是何氏的始祖祠，融汇元明清不同画风，是粤中宗祠文化的代表作。清雅典丽的三稔厅是清末"何氏三杰"何柳堂、何少霞、何与年演奏之所，三杰开创了广东音乐何氏典雅派，他们创作的《雨打芭蕉》《赛龙夺锦》等名曲享誉世界。飘色是沙湾最独特的民间艺术，融戏剧、杂技、歌舞于一炉，鲜艳夺目的小演员凌空而立、翩然似仙，令人叹为观止。

Located in Panyu District, Guangzhou City, Shawan Ancient Town was first built during the Southern Song Dynasty. Originally an ancient sea bay, it has gradually become land after generations of embankment and reclamation. During the Ming and Qing dynasties, it accommodated "tens of thousands of households". Following the green stone streets and alleys into the ancient town, you will first set eyes on the smoothly beautiful and towering wok-ear-shaped walls, which feature distinct Guangdong characteristics. The wok-ear-shaped walls are like an official hat in ancient China, implying "to come first in the imperial civil examination at the highest level". They used to be symbols of status and wealth. Numerous majestic wok-ear-walled mansions reveal the past glory of Shawan. What reveals a greater sense of ingenuity is the oyster shell wall with the impression of a sculpture. An oyster shell wall is not only firm and beautiful but also water-proof and worm-repellant. Besides, it makes a house warm in winter and cool in summer. Most of the residents in the ancient town are surnamed He, with the majestic and solemn Liugeng Hall being the Temple of the First Ancestors of the He's Clan. Incorporating different paintings styles of the Yuan, Ming, and Qing dynasties, it is a representative work of the ancestral temple culture of central Guangdong. The refined, elegant, and beautiful Sannian (Three Harvests) Hall is the venue of performance for the Three Outstanding Figures of the He's Clan, including He Liutang (1872–1933), He Shaoxia (1894–1942), and He Yunian (1880–1962). They created the He's Elegant School of Guangdong Music, with their self-created tunes such as *Raindrops Rattling on Banana Leaves* and *A Race of Dragon Boats for the Champion* enjoying worldwide fame. As the most unique folk art in Shawa, *Piaose* incorporates drama, acrobatics, songs and dances. On the performance, young and brightly dressed performers are high up in the air, looking like fluttering immortals, presenting a spectacular sight.

大鹏所城：海防要塞，名将之村
Dapeng Fortress: Strategic Stronghold for Coastal Defense and Village of Famous Generals

大鹏所城巍然矗立于广东深圳市碧海之畔，已有六百余载。古城全称为"大鹏守御千户所城"，是明朝为抗倭而设的海防要塞，清朝时因在九龙海战中大败英军而名垂史册。深圳别称"鹏城"，即源自于此。古城明清风貌犹存，雄伟古老的城墙虽苔痕斑驳却气势不减，如威风赫赫的沙场老将。古迹中以赖恩爵的将军府保存得最为完好。因赖恩爵在鸦片战争首战中大扬国威，痛击英国侵略者，道光皇帝赐建此府，并御笔亲书"振威将军第"作为门首横额。清朝水师名将刘起龙的将军府亦保存完好、格局如旧。清朝赖氏"三代五将"和刘氏"父子将军"至今传为美谈，明清两朝大鹏所城共出过十几位将军，"将军村"可谓实至名归。行走其间，遥想当年水军将士们御敌报国的鲲鹏之志，心潮澎湃。

Towering beside the blue sea of Shenzhen City, Guangdong, Dapeng Fortress has a history of over six hundred years. With its full name of "Dapeng Independent Battalion City", it was a strategic stronghold for coastal defense against Japanese pirates in the Ming Dynasty. In the Qing Dynasty, it witnessed the great defeat of the British troops in the Battle of Kowloon, leaving its name on the roll of fame. Shenzhen's alternative name Pengcheng was originated from this. The ancient city's features of the Ming and Qing dynasties have been preserved, in which the majestic and old city walls, despite being mottled, have maintained their imposing demeanors as battle-hardened generals with majestic looks. Among the ancient relics, General Lai Enjue's Mansion is the best preserved. As he dealt a heavy blow on the British troops and revealed China's national power and influence during the first battle of the Opium War (1840–1842), Emperor Daoguang bestowed this mansion to him and personally inscribed it with the words of "Mansion of General Might-Revealing" as the horizontal scroll of the gate. The General's Mansion of Liu Qilong (1772–1830), a famous general of the navy of the Qing Dynasty, has also been

well preserved, with its ancient pattern. The "five generals in three generations" of the Lai Clan and the "father and son as generals" of the Liu Clan in the Qing Dynasty have been stories passed on with approval. During the Ming and Qing dynasties, Dapeng Suocheng City witnessed the emergence of dozens of generals, making the fame of "the village of generals" live up to reality. Walking in the ancient city, you will feel an upsurge of emotions by thinking of the lofty ideals of the soldiers and generals in the navy as they resisted enemies and defended the country.

07 吴阳：东海朝阳，状元故里
Wuyang: Hometown of the Top Successful Candidate of the Imperial Examination at the Highest Level, with the Sunrise Scene on the Eastern Sea

吴阳古镇隶属广东吴川市，东濒南海、西襟鉴江，自隋朝至民国为吴川县治所在地达一千三百多年。吴阳地处鉴江出海口，芷寮古港曾繁华千年，明朝时为粤西著名商埠，商贾云集、帆樯数里，当时有"金芷寮，银赤坎"之说。时光煮雨，清末古港已衰，唯其特产芷寮蟹、沙螺美名远扬。吴阳自古文运昌隆、才俊辈出，其名最显者为清朝状元林召棠，他的故居至今保存完好，乡人皆以"状元故里"为傲。始建于元代的吴川学宫碧瓦雕甍、重檐翘角，曾培养过林召棠、陈兰彬等名士。城南河畔的极浦亭始建于南宋，是解元李凌云隐居讲学之所。亭前原为江面宽广的河湾，鉴水清波绕门而过，夕阳西下归帆点点，一派渔歌唱晚的怡人风光。"玉笔凌霄"的双峰塔依山面海而立，已有四百余年。吴阳有十八千米水清沙幼的黄金海岸线，日出日落霞光满天、绮丽万端，"东海朝阳"是亘古未变的吴阳胜景。

Under the jurisdiction of Wuchuan City, Guangdong, Wuyang Ancient Town is on the bank of the South China Sea to its east and adjacent to the Jianjiang River to its west. It had been the seat of Wuchuan County for over 1,300 years from the Sui Dynasty to the period of the Republic of China. Located on the estuary of the Jianjiang River, Wujiang had the Zhiliao Ancient Port which had been prosperous for thousands of years. During the Ming Dynasty, it was a famous commercial port in western Guangdong, with merchants gathering in crowds and sails stretching for miles. There was a notion of "Zhiliao of gold and Chikan of silver". With the passage of time, the ancient port in the final years of the Qing Dynasty had declined, leaving behind only its specialties such as Zhiliao crabs and sand spiral shells enjoying fame far and wide. Since ancient times, Wuyang has been culturally prosperous, with talents coming forth in great numbers. The most renowned one of them was Lin Zhaotang (1786–1872), the top successful candidate of the imperial civil examination of the highest level in the Qing Dynasty. His former residence, which has been well preserved, has been hailed as the "hometown of the top successful candidate of the imperial civil examination at the highest level". First built in the Yuan Dynasty, the Wuchuan Academy features green roof tiles, carved beams, overlapping eaves, and overhanging cornices, having witnessed the emergence of such famous figures such as Lin Zhaotang (1786–1873, an ancient Chinese official) and Chen Lanbin (1816–1895, an ancient Chinese official). Located on the river bank on the south of the city, the Jipu Pavilion was first built in the Southern Song Dynasty and used by Li Lingyun (around the 13th century), a first-placed candidate in the provincial imperial civil examination, as he lived and lectured in seclusion. Before the Pavilion is a river bay with a vast river surface. The clear waves of the Jianshui River roll past before gates. Under the setting sun, the river is dotted with sails on their returning trips, presenting a pleasant landscape with fishermen's songs sung at dusk. The Shuangfeng (Double Peaks) Pagoda, hailed as "a jade pen rising high into the sky", has already been towering beside the mountain and the sea for over four centuries. Wuyang is also featured by a golden coast with eighteen kilometers of clear water and fine sand. In sunrise and sunset, the sun cast resplendent rays all over the sky. "The Sunrise Scene of the Eastern Sea" has been a famous scenery in Wuyang from time immemorial.

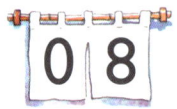

08 松口：南洋首站，客家侨乡
Songkou: First Stop to Southeast Asia and Hometown of Overseas Hakka People

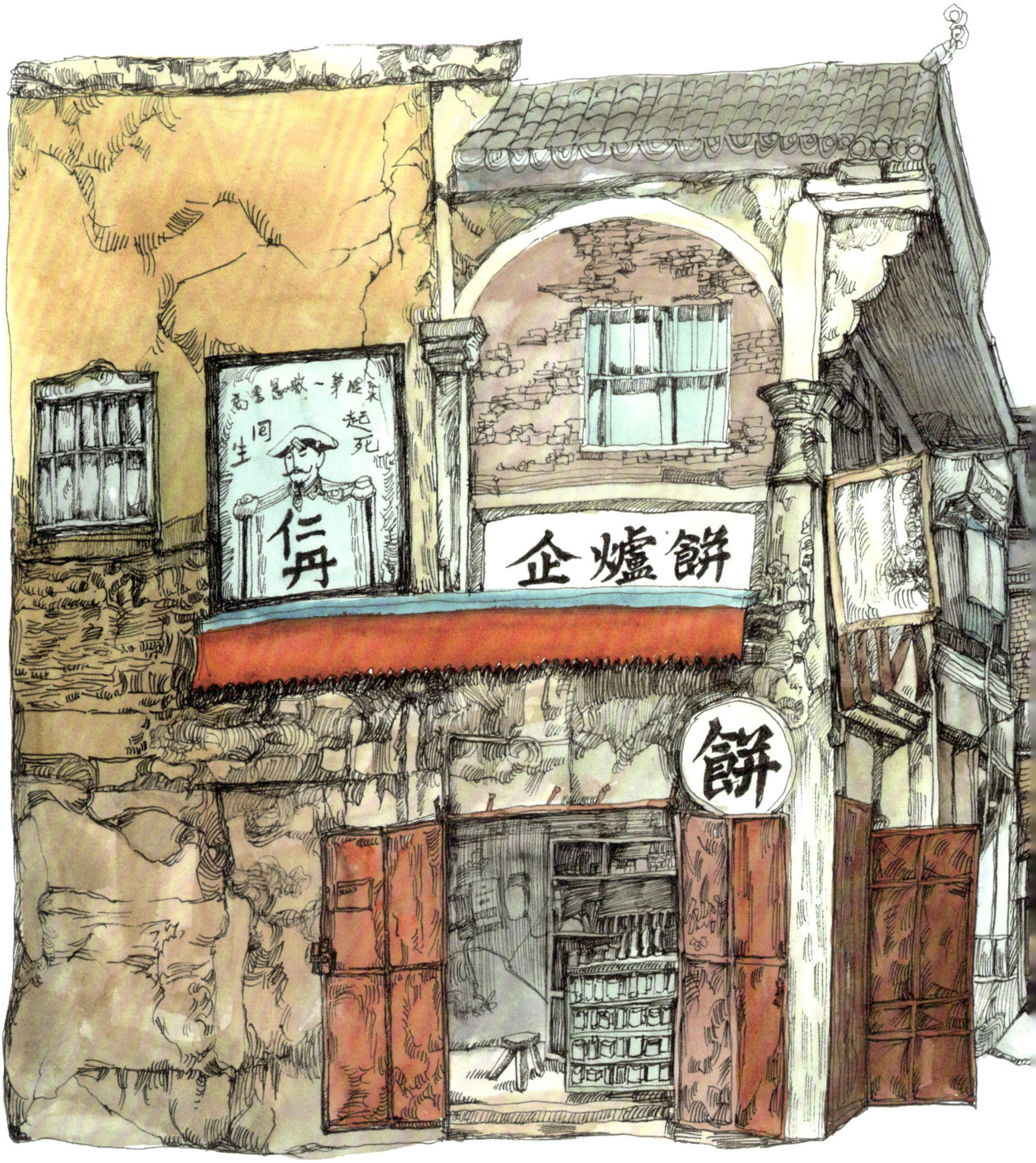

广东梅州市松口古镇地处闽粤赣交会要冲，梅江穿城而过，因水陆两便，自古是粤东商贸名镇，曾享千年繁华。松口是客家重镇，也是著名侨乡，清末民初曾有数万客家人从这里登船，经"海上丝绸之路"下南洋淘金。百转千回的客家山歌唱尽了百年前的离别相思。创业有成、衣锦荣归的侨民在家乡留下无数华屋洋楼，造就了松口中西合璧、古今结合的侨乡风情。走在松口古街上，南洋风情的灰塑骑楼错落连绵，古朴斑驳的木板铺面亦不少见。气派恢宏的松江大酒店是民国时梅州最高档的旅店，见证了无数华侨眷属的悲欢离合。松口华侨作为旧中国睁眼看世界的第一群人，始终不忘桑梓、心系救国。承德楼的主人梁密庵、爱春楼的主人谢逸桥，都是资助辛亥革命的著名侨商。革命成功后，孙中山曾亲临松口，与爱国华侨留下了珍贵的合影。

Located in Meizhou City of Guangdong Province, Songkou Ancient Town is at a strategic junction of Fujian, Guangdong, and Guangxi. With the Meijiang River flowing through the ancient town, it features convenient water and land transport conditions. It has been a famous commercial town in eastern Guangdong Province since ancient times, with its prosperity lasting for thousands of years. Songkou is a significant town for the Hakka people and a famous hometown for overseas Chinese. In the late Qing Dynasty and the early period of the Republic of China, tens of thousands of Hakka people boarded ships here to ferry through the "Maritime Silk Road" to Southeast Asia to seek fortunes. The folk songs of the Hakka people, which feature melodies full of twists and turns, fully express the parting griefs and yearnings over one hundred years ago. The overseas Chinese, who had made achievements and returned home with acquired wealth and honor, had left behind numerous magnificent residences including some Western-style buildings, giving rise to the conditions and customs of Songkou as a hometown of overseas Chinese which merges the elements of China and the West and the present and the ancient. Strolling on the ancient street of Songkou, you will see undulating grey arcade buildings, which are rich in the conditions and customs of Southeast Asia, in attractive disorder. The antiquely simplistic and mottled wooden shop and store facades are also commonly seen. The majestic Songjiang Grand Hotel, which is the highest-grade hotel in Meizhou during the period of the Republic of China, witnessed the partings and reunions of numerous overseas Chinese and their family members. The overseas Chinese of Songkou, as the first group of people who opened their eyes to the world in old China, have been concerned with their hometown and saving China. Liang Mi'an (1880–1940, owner of Chengde Building) and Xie Yiqiao (1874–1926, owner of the Aichun Building), were famous overseas merchants who funded the Xinhai Revolution in 1911 (which ended the feudal rule in China). After the success of the revolution, Sun Yat-sen (1866–1925, leader of the Xinhai Revolution in 1911 and first president of the Republic of China) went personally to Songkou to take precious photos with patriotic overseas Chinese.

第八章
Chapter 8

八闽福地

Blessed Lands of Fujian Province

长汀：客家首府，红色山城
Changting: Principal City of the Hakka People and Revolution-Themed Mountainous City

福建长汀古城地处武夷山南麓，为闽粤赣三省边陲要冲。汉代置县，唐代设汀州，成为福建五大州之一。始建于大唐的古城墙枕山临溪设十二座城门，遥望如一串佛珠挂于卧龙山，气象雄浑、古韵悠长。长汀是客家首府，绕城而过的汀江被喻为客家人的母亲河，古城至今保存着不少宋代以来的客家古民居，它继承了中原府第式建筑风格，布局严谨、精致典雅。古朴的云骧阁是福建苏维埃政府旧址，在明清两朝是汀州试院，院中两株唐代巨柏依旧黛色参天、荫庇千年。雕饰精美的天后宫静立数百年，散发着宋代建筑清雅柔逸的气息。长汀是近代红色革命的重要发祥地，位于金沙河西岸的辛耕别墅曾是红四军的司令部，毛泽东和朱德都住过这里。罗汉岭是1935年瞿秋白英勇就义之地，如今在这块浸染着烈士鲜血的土地上竖立了英雄纪念碑，家国情怀世代相传。

Located on the southern foot of the Wuyi Mountain in Fujian Province, Changting Ancient City is a strategic borderland of Fujian, Guangdong, and Guangxi. Established as a county in the Han Dynasty, it was set up as the Tingzhou Prefecture in the Tang Dynasty, making itself one of the five major prefectures in Fujian. The ancient city walls, first built in the Tang Dynasty, are beside hills and streams. Its twelve city gates, when looked at a distance, are like a string of Buddhist beads on the Wolong (Hidden Dragon) Mountain. They reveal a majestic demeanor and a lasting antique appeal. Changting is the principal city of the Hakka people, while the Tingjiang River which flows through the city is hailed as the mother river of the Hakka people. Preserved in the ancient city are a number of ancient residential buildings of the Hakka people since the Song Dynasty, which have inherited the mansion-type architectural style of the Central Plains with their rigorous layouts and exquisite and refined features. The antiquely simplistic Yunxiang (Cloud and Horse) Pavilion is the former site of the Chinese Soviet Government of Fujian. During the Ming and Qing dynasties, it was the venue of the imperial civil examination in the Tingzhou Prefecture. In its courtyard are two giant cypress trees planted in the Tang Dynasty. With its dark green foliage and towering height, it has offered shade and shelter for thousands of years. The Tianhou (Heavenly Empress) Palace, with its exquisite carvings and other ornaments, have been standing in tranquility for centuries, sending forth the

refined, elegant, mild, and relaxing favor of buildings from the Song Dynasty. Changting was a significant place of origin for the red revolution, with the Xingeng (Diligent Farming) Villa being the headquarters of No.4 Red Army and the dwellings for Mao Zedong (1893–1976, Chinese communist leader and first president of the PRC) and Zhu De (1886–1976, Chinese communist leader and founder of the People's Liberation Army). The Luohan (Arhats) Ridge witnessed the heroic death of Qu Qiubai (1899–1935, a Chinese politician). At present, a heroes' monument has been set up on this land soaked with martyrs' blood, with the affections for families and the nation passed on generation after generation.

02 和平：卵石城堡，进士之乡
Heping: A Castle of Pebbles and a Hometown of Successful Candidates of the Imperial Civil Examinations at the Highest Level

和平是福建邵武南部一座千年城堡古镇，也是太极宗师张三丰的故里。和平，古称"禾坪"，意为种稻谷良田平坦开阔之地。贯穿古镇南北的旧市街，又名昼锦街，唐代已是人烟稠密、繁华似锦，被誉为"福建第一街"。走在街上，大唐的马蹄声似隐隐从光亮如镜的青石板下传来，氤氲数百年的游浆豆腐的芬芳依旧沁人心脾。阡陌纵横的卵石街巷中两百余间明清民居星罗棋布，数幢斗拱层叠的豪门巨宅气势非凡。大门状如官帽的和平书院传承千年书香，自开科取士以来，共培养进士一百三十七名，为和平赢得"进士之乡"之誉。李士大夫第华美无匹，此门李氏清末"一门九大夫"，巧夺天工的砖雕艺术彰显了主人的尊贵身份。为御匪患，明代和平人就地取材，以河卵石砌筑城墙，建起了独具特色的卵石城堡。当年设立的四座谯楼仍有其二屹立城墙之上，数百年来看惯云卷云舒兴衰之变。

　　Located on the south of Shaowu in Fujian Province, Heping Ancient Town is a millennium-old castle-style town. It is the hometown of Zhang Sanfeng (1247-?, an ancient Chinese Taoist and the founder of Taijiquan Boxing), the patriarch of the theory of *Taiji* (Supreme Ultimate). Heping (Peace) was known as Heping (Flatland of Grain Seeding) in ancient times, referring to flat and wide land with paddy fields. The ancient street, also known as the Zhoujin (Daylight Brocade) Street, runs from north to south of the ancient town. In the Tang Dynasty, it was already a densely populated town as flourishing as brocade. Strolling on the street, you will seem to be hearing the hoofbeats of the Tang Dynasty from the mirror-bright green stone slabs. The Youjiang (smoothly flowing thick liquid) tofu, which has been made for centuries, is still exuding a mentally refreshing fragrance. On the crisscrossing pebble streets and alleys, over two hundred residential buildings from the Ming Dynasty are scattered all over like stars in the sky or chess pieces on a chessboard. Several large-scale mansions with overlapping *Dougong* (corbel brackets) reveal extraordinary manners. The Heping Academy, featuring a gate that looks like an ancient Chinese official's hat, has passed on its literary reputation for thousands of years. Since the start of selecting officials through the imperial civil examinations, it had cultivated 137 successful candidates of the imperial civil examinations at the highest level, earning the reputation of "the hometown of successful candidates of the imperial civil examinations at the highest level". The mansion of the Li Clan is exceptionally magnificent. In the late years of the Qing Dynasty, the Li Clan witnessed the emergence of "nine ministers". The brick carving art, characterized by the wonderful workmanship excelling Nature, has revealed the esteemed status of its owners. To resist bandits in the Ming Dynasty, the people of Heping utilized local materials of pebbles to construct the town walls and set up a distinctly featured pebble castle. Among the four watchtowers built back then, two are still towering on the town walls, witnessing the town's ups and downs for centuries.

03 湖坑：土楼之乡，山居神话
Hukeng: A Hometown of *Tulou* and a Legend of Living in Mountains

湖坑镇隶属福建龙岩市永定区，是世界文化遗产——福建土楼的核心所在地。古镇依山傍水，登高远眺，只见悠悠南溪穿过狭长山谷，两岸百余座形态各异的土楼镶嵌于层叠梯田、弯曲溪岸上，宛若游龙蜿蜒二十余里，构成"土楼长城"的壮美风景。圆形土楼最为经典，圆中圆、圈套圈，俯瞰如拔地而起的巨型蘑菇，又如从天而降的神秘飞碟，独特造型曾惊艳西方世界。土楼是福建客家人独有的建筑形式，其内屋舍密布，数百人聚族而居，既便于安全防御，也反映了客家人孝悌和睦的伦理传统。镇中的洪坑明清土楼群很早就蜚声海外。富丽堂皇的振成楼外观酷似乌纱帽，主体呈八卦布局，"外土内洋、中西合璧"的风格世所罕见。高贵典雅的福裕楼飞檐翘角层层叠落如凤凰展翅，是五凤楼的典范之作。雄伟的奎聚楼是依山而筑的宫殿式方形土楼，楼宇参差、错落有致，远观势如布达拉宫。

Under the jurisdiction of Yongding District, Longyan City, Fujian Province, Hukeng Town is in the core area of Fujian *Tulou* in the world heritage list. The ancient town was built beside mountains and waters. After ascending a height to look into the distance, you will see the Nanxi Stream meandering gently through a narrow and long valley. On both banks are over one hundred *Tulou* of various shapes embedded on layers of terraced fields and winding stream banks. Like a swimming dragon, they wind along a journey of over 20 li, constituting a magnificent view of "the Great Wall of Tulou". Among them, the circular *Tulou* are the most classic ones featuring circles inside circles. Looking down from a height, you will find that they look like giant mushrooms rising steeply from the level ground or mysterious flying saucers which descended from outer space. Their unique forms have amazed the West. As an architectural style unique to the Hakka people in Fujian Province, *Tulou* feature densely arranged houses inside, where hundreds of people of the same clan live together, making it easy for security defense and reflecting the filial piety, fraternal duties, and good neighborliness of the Hakka people. The *Tulou* of the Ming and Qing dynasties in Hongkeng in the town have long been renowned in China and abroad. The beautiful and imposing Zhencheng Building strikingly resembles a black hat worn by an ancient Chinese official. Its main part reveals a layout of eight trigrams. Its style with "external local features and internal Western characteristics" combining Chinese and Western elements is a rarity around the world. The noble elegant Fuyu (Blessings and Affluence) Building, with its overlapping eaves and cornices, is like a phoenix fluttering its wings. The magnificent Kuiju Building is a palace-style square Tulou. With its houses in attractive disorder, it is as majestic as the Potala Palace.

04 塔下：南国之靖，太极水乡
Taxia: A Peaceful Land in Southern China and a Waterside Town Featuring Taiji (Supreme Ultimate)

　　塔下村坐落于福建南靖县的高山峡谷中，四面群峰竞秀、积翠凝岚，一道清澈闪亮的溪水呈 S 形蜿蜒流过，串起两岸四十余座高大雄浑的客家土楼，构成一幅清丽绝妙的太极水乡图。塔下土楼有方形、圆形、围裙形、曲尺形，造型各异、蔚为大观，溪畔还伫立若干单院式吊脚楼，形成了大楼带小楼、高低错落布局的奇妙景观。塔下历史可追溯至元末明初，客家先祖迁居南国不忘中原文化，始建于乾隆年间的张氏宗祠德远堂传递着忠孝伦理，堂前的二十四根石龙旗杆是客家人"诗礼传家"的象征。距塔下不远的裕昌楼构造奇特，横梁东倒西斜却屹立七百年不倒，至今仍有人居，堪称建筑奇迹。附近的田螺坑土楼群亦以神奇造型闻名遐迩，翠竹绿林中四座圆楼环绕一座方楼，登高俯瞰形如"四菜一汤"一桌菜，甚为有趣。

　　Located in a valley of high mountains in Nanjing County of Fujian Province, Taxia Village is surrounded by peaks vying in their beauty and green trees amid the mist. A glitteringly lucid stream meanders in an S shape through the village, connecting over forty tall and majestic *Tulou* of the Hakka people on both banks and constituting a quiet, exquisite, and exceptional waterside town scroll featuring the Taoist concept of Taiji (Supreme Ultimate). In Taxia Village stand various shapes of Tulou, including square, circular, apron-shaped and set-square-shaped ones. Of various forms, they present a splendid sight. On the stream's banks are some pillar-supported buildings with detached courtyards, forming a wonderful view of large buildings taking small ones and all buildings in attractive disorder vertically and horizontally. The history of Taxia Village traces back to the late years of the Yuan Dynasty and the early years of the Ming Dynasty (in mid 14th century). The ancestors of the Hakka people, after relocating to Southern China, still kept the culture of the Central Plains in mind. The Ancestral Temple of the Zhang's Clan, also known as the Deyuan (Spreading Virtue) Hall, which was built in the years of Emperor Qianlong (r. 1735–1799), conveys the ethics of loyalty and filial piety. Before the hall are 24 flagpoles with patterns of dragons, which are symbols of "passing on the family lineage with learning and etiquettes". Not far from Taxia Village is the Yuchang (Affluence and Prosperity) Building featuring a unique structure. Despite its rickety crossbeams, it has been stood erect for seven centuries and was dwelled till now, deserving to be hailed as an architectural miracle. Not far from it is the Tianluokeng *Tulou* cluster with a widespread reputation for its magical form. Amid the emerald forest of bamboos is a square *Tulou* with four circular buildings. After ascending a height to look down, you will find that it looks amusingly like a table of dishes with four entrees and a soup.

05 芷溪：客家大宅，祠居合一
Zhixi: Mansions of the Hakka People Used as Temples and Residential Buildings

福建连城县芷溪村坐落于冠豸山与梅花山之间的盆地之中，清清芷水绕村而流，古时溪畔长满芬芳芷草，"芷溪"由此得名。古村悠悠千载，清代发展为万人客家大村，人曰"千烟之家"。明清以降，芷溪先民先后建了七十四座古宗祠、一百三十八幢古民居，其中多数是祠居合一的复合型建筑，普遍采用"九厅十八井"结构布局，气势恢宏、彩饰辉煌，被誉为"客家大宅门"。巍峨华赡的黄氏家庙雄踞山腰数百年，不论寒暑，祠内从无蜘蛛蚊蚋，堪称一奇。琉瓦飞檐的翠畴公祠是客家围屋风格，其雕塑彩绘之精湛在闽西数一数二。古雅大气的集鳣堂历经三百年风雨至今仍有人居住，府上楹联匾额多为何绍基、林则徐等名士真迹。宗祠文化的昌盛，反映了客家人慎终追远、敬祖睦宗的传统。每年正月，晶莹剔透的芷溪花灯长龙走街入巷，配以苏州锣鼓和十番音乐，明烛夜空、古韵悠长，是一道传承三百年的佳节夜景。

Under the jurisdiction of Liancheng County in Fujian Province, Zhixi Village is located in the basin between Guanzhai Mountain and Meihua Mountain. The lucid Zhixi Stream flows around the village. In ancient times, the banks of the stream were overgrown with fragrant *Zhi* (angelica), which gave rise to the name of "Zhixi Stream". The ancient village features a millennium-old history. In the Qing Dynasty, it developed into a major village with over 10,000 people in "thousands of households". Since the start of the Ming and Qing dynasties, the ancestors in the Zhixi Village had built 74 ancient ancestral temples and 138 ancient residential buildings, among which are composite buildings used as temples and residential buildings at the same time. These buildings have witnessed the common use of the structural pattern of "multiple halls and yards". With their majestic manners and magnificent colorful ornaments, they are hailed as the "great mansions of the Hakka people". The Temple of the Huang's Clan, characterized by its towering, imposing, and magnificent look, has been located prominently on the mountainside for centuries. Throughout all seasons, the temple has no spiders, mosquitoes, and other insects, which can be hailed as a miracle. Featuring its glazed tiles and overhanging eaves, Lord Cuichou's Temple is of the enclosed building style of the Hakka people. Its exquisite sculptures and colorful paintings are reckoned to be the top in western Fujian. The antique, elegant, and majestic Jizhan (Sturgeon-Gathering)

Hall, after enduring three centuries of vicissitude, is still inhabited today. The couplets and horizontal scrolls in the mansion have mostly been the genuine works of He Shaoji (1799–1883, an ancient Chinese painter and calligrapher), Lin Zexu (1785–1850, an ancient Chinese official), and other renowned figures. The prosperous ancestral temple culture reflects the Hakka people's tradition to pay close attention to the funerary rites to one's parents and the sacrificing rites to one's ancestors, to respect one's ancestors, and to get amicable with one's clan. In the first lunar month each year, the glittering and translucent long colored lantern dragon makes rounds of streets and alleys, accompanied by the gongs, drums, and *Shifan* (ensemble of ten traditional percussion instruments) music. With brightly lit candles illuminating the night sky amid lingering antique appeal, it presents the nightscape of a fine festival that has been passed on for three centuries.

Ancient Chinese Towns

Written by Liu Ying

Illustrated by Zhao Nan and Huang Zexin

First English Edition 2023

By China Pictorial Press Co., Ltd.

CHINA INTERNATIONAL COMMUNICATIONS GROUP

Copyright © China Pictorial Press Co., Ltd.

All rights reserved.

No part of this publication may be reproduced, stored in a retrieval system, or transmitted in any form or by any means, electronic, mechanical, photocopying, recording, or otherwise, without the prior written permission of China Pictorial Press Co., Ltd., except for the inclusion of brief quotations in an acknowledged review.

Address: 33 Chegongzhuang Xilu, Haidian District, Beijing, 100048, China

ISBN 978-7-5146-2069-6